The Moth Comes to the Flame

Conversations Between Seeker and Sage

Volume Two

The Moth Comes to the Flame

Conversations Between Seeker and Sage

Volume Two

By John Roberts

Roaring Lion Publishing Company

The Moth Comes to the Flame
Volume Two
can be purchased in retail stores or by mail from:

Roaring Lion Publishing Company
P.O. Box 471
Boise, Idaho 83701

Visa or Mastercard orders call
1-800-358-1929

Please add $4.00 shipping and handling for all orders. Idaho residents add $1.25 sales tax.

Written by John Roberts
Editing and Text Layout by Carol Lyons
Cover Design by Neil Marwehe
Cover Art by Marie-Claude Sontag

No part of this book may be used in any manner whatsoever without written permission from the publisher except in the case of brief quotations embodied in critical articles and reviews.
©John Allan Roberts

First Edition - 1998

ISBN 1-878682-04-0 : $25.00

Library of Congress Card Number 98-092155

To Peter,

Whom I regard with love, awe and admiration.
You are a living example of truth, wisdom,
health and a loving heart.
I thank you for being my friend.
You take me to higher planes of consciousness;
to peaks of grandeur, to the top of the mountain.
Because of you, I am so much more —
a moth who has found the flame.

Table of Contents

Mind

Are You Aware and Conscious?	3
Developing Intuition	17
Dreams	25
The Need for Clarity	33
The Power of Thought	45

Health

Healing Yourself	77
What Causes Accidents and Illnesses?	113
Food and Health	135
Health and Sexuality	171
The Effects of the Environment	191
Longevity and Immortality	203

Wealth

Creating Wealth	237
The Way to Success	259
Decisions Bring Solutions	271
The Need for Choices	281
Work	287
Responsibility	297
The ABCs of Wealth	309
Five Self-Sabotages that Prevent Prosperity	317
Generosity	339

Spirituality

The Nature of God	345
Masters and Mastery	355
Meditation	383
Transformation	413
Enlightenment	427

FORWARD

You hold in your hands a book of great beauty and power. If you take its message to heart, it will surely change your life. The following conversations form a most unusual dialogue. John Roberts has deftly woven the illuminating perceptions of life given to him by a mysterious man called Peter. Peter is a remarkable individual. He is an authentic American sage.

I consider it a privilege to know Peter. When I first met him, I realized I was face to face with a man who might best be described by that overused word — *enlightened*. Peter's approach to the mystery is built on the ancient sacred traditions, yet is refreshingly modern. His emphasis is on self-mastery and liberation, not obedience.

This book will appeal to those who have no wish to submit to new doctrines, but desire the joy and expansiveness of true realization and self-mastery. Peter will likely challenge your current beliefs about what is possible. Perhaps he will lead you beyond where you have dared walk before. He just might cause an earthquake inside you. At the very least, Peter will give you a glimpse of a more luminous way of thinking and living.

It's tempting to use glossy adjectives and hyped-up superlatives to describe Peter. But that would not convey a clear picture of his uniqueness. The measure of a human being is not simply one's philosophy. It's how one lives that is the real yardstick of one's character and spirituality. In *The Moth Comes to the Flame,* you will get to know Peter through his illuminating thoughts. Through John Roberts you will share glimpses into Peter's personal life and spiritual practice. In addition, I think it would also help you to better understand Peter if I offered a few anecdotes gathered by his friends.

Many incidents in Peter's life sound like they come from a fairy tale. Peter and Ann live beside a large forest in eastern Tennessee. One day, Peter was walking alone through the forest when he came upon a large female black bear that was soon to give birth. One can imagine what a delicate situation this would be! Unafraid, Peter gently spoke reassuring words to the bear and then lay down on his back in the forest. He let the bear sniff him, all the while speaking gently and comfortingly to her. Weeks later the bear — now a mother — came bounding proudly to Peter's house, with her newborn cubs trailing behind. Naturally, she wanted to show Peter her cubs! (Note: There is a photo in The Magic Man *of Peter babysitting the cubs while the mother is sticking her head in the door of Peter's bedroom.)*

Since that time, Peter's forest home has become a destination for the bears — a veritable "social hub" for the four-leggeds. At times, as many as 15-20 bears sleep on his and Ann's deck each night. Deer and bear are sometimes seen in amicable proximity to each other near their home — a situation not common in nature's pattern.

Peter is so physically strong that he can bend iron horseshoes, nails, and steel spikes with his bare hands the way most people might bend a coat hanger. Yet he is so gentle that animals in the wild show no fear around him. Once he picked up a poisonous copperhead, then set it softly back in the grass a considerable distance from the house. When he and his friends disturbed a yellow jacket's nest, everyone ran to escape the angry bees. All except Peter, who gazed at them like a fascinated child without once getting stung. Even insects, it seems, recognize a gentle, loving heart. Where there is only love, fear vanishes.

Peter has healed many people. Once he laid his hands on a young boy's broken foot. After a few moments the boy exclaimed that he could feel the bones moving! In a matter of minutes he threw away his crutches and walked. Peter's world is interwoven with the magical and the miraculous. People have witnessed him raise his hands and make heavy clouds disperse, letting sunlight stream through. Once when he and his friends were building his home on a mountaintop in the Smoky Mountains, it was raining heavily all around them. Although the roof was not yet built, Peter insisted they continue despite the rain, saying, "It's not going to rain on us; keep working." Sure enough, it showered constantly for hours all around them, yet no rain fell on the house.

Peter is the healthiest person I have ever met. He has taken nutrition into the realm of spiritual alchemy, using it as a means to transform and regenerate the soul and the body. Peter appears to be essentially ageless. He honors the body as the physical temple of the spirit. Knowing Peter, I'm beginning to have to admit that maybe, just maybe, it really is possible to live forever in a physical body.

If you've been around the spiritual supermarket as long as I have, you've no doubt seen some odd spectacles. Unlike pseudospiritual teachers, Peter is very balanced and grounded. He doesn't make extravagant claims, and refrains from indulging in what might be called "metaphysical mumbo jumbo" — far-fetched speculation that cannot be verified. Rather, he emphasizes the importance of accountability and achievement in daily life.

It's likely that all of us feel a little jaded when we hear of so-called spiritual masters who can talk a good game but fail to live up to their words. Peter is genuine. He lives his message and walks his talk. Yet don't try to make him your guru. If you tried to bow down at his "lotus feet" he might just give you a soft kick. Peter emphasizes taking charge of one's own life. That's refreshing in an age when many false prophets seek recognition and adulation.

Peter has a vast and detailed knowledge of the world's wisdom traditions, those of the East as well as the West. His approach is refreshingly balanced, gracefully harmonizing various spiritual perspectives. Peter emphasizes the importance of creating a beautiful environment that reflects the spirit and manifests sacred space. In this regard, he stands out in stark contrast to many *sadhus,* or holy men of the East, who disregard the cleanliness of their bodies and the value of their physical environment. Peter talks freely and frankly about money and prosperity. He reminds us that wealth is the natural state of our inner selves and that it's all right to live abundantly. Peter himself is an author, successful businessman and entrepreneur.

Peter can speak eloquently for days on a wide range of topics, from economics to history, and from health to the secrets of spiritual understanding. He loves to laugh, and is not ashamed to weep at the expression of something beautiful. Perhaps what moves Peter the most is to see human beings surpassing themselves, living courageously and opening up the full powers within them.

Despite Peter's obvious mastery in countless areas, I'm certain that he is very much like all of us. It's just that he has uncovered more of his "specialness" than have most of us. In most people, that "specialness" lies buried under a veneer of false beliefs, wrong assumptions, and the residue of past failures. Peter gently helps us remove those false perceptions about who we are. The shining spirit within us can then stand free.

All really authentic teachers believe profoundly in the freedom of the human spirit. Peter loves freedom and he wants to share the freedom he has found with those wise enough to seek the truth. Our minds love to complicate things. The intellect seeks the most intricate and complex of answers. Perhaps this is because intellectual complexity appeals to our vanity. Life is not always easy. But solving many of life's dilemmas may be much simpler than we allow. The heart grants clarity and simplicity, enabling us to see the truth reflected like sunlight on peaceful waters. Peter always brings us gently back to the primacy of the heart.

If Peter demonstrates more mastery than you or I, he offers that as evidence of what we may become. Peter would be the first to say that all the beauty, all the love, and all the happiness that we seek resides within our own minds, hearts and deeper selves. For those who feel the call to surpass themselves and to touch the divine spark in their hearts, Peter is there as a living model. Take him as a signpost. But as he would say, don't worship the signpost.

Oh, and let me include this word of warning. If you are egotistical, vain, or narrow-minded, you might as well stop right here. Peter will only offend you. If you are filled to the brim with other people's belief systems that you have unquestioningly swallowed from childhood on,

Peter is likely to cause a tempest in your mind. But if you are flexible and truly looking for peace, serenity, and a bright lantern for the journey, you hold a treasure in your hands.

Peter has found the solution to life's problems. Let John Roberts share those insights with you. You are about to partake of a feast. This is food for the spirit that can guide you to a happier and more fulfilling life. *The Moth Comes to the Flame* is a conversation with an illumined soul. It can be read as if it were a dialogue with your own higher self. John Roberts' writing is as lucid as lightning on a dark night and as refreshing as rain drops in midsummer. Let this book be a new friend in your life. Each thought that becomes a part of you will be a new force in your soul. Take possession of these ideas and make them your own. Put them into practice and you will change your destiny.

This book is a road map into the kingdom of the new consciousness. Open your mind to these truths and you'll begin a journey that leads to the center of your heart. There you'll discover the key to happiness, power, and heavenly joy. These insights will help you find your way home.

Emory John Michael

Author of *Queen of the Sun*
and *The Alchemy of Sacred Living*

Acknowledgments

To the following friends who were such incredible readers, critiquing and praising every page, I thank you so much. I am grateful that you were a part of the process.

> Gay Whitesides Paula Jones
> Nancy Budge Paula Hull
> Barbara Knudson Chris Binion
> Bonnie Vestal Mike Piccirilli

To Janice Wittenborn, I will be forever grateful for her tenacious, even relentless, urging to get me to attend my first seminar with Peter in October, 1991.

To Carol Lyons, for taking the words from these seminars and creating the format and final layout, as well as working extensively on the copy editing.

To Emory John Michael, for writing the forward.

To Marie-Claude Sontag, for allowing me to use her award-winning, watercolor portrait of Peter on the cover.

To Neil Marwehe, for cover design.

To Jo-Ann Langseth, who worked diligently on the final copy editing.

To Lorry Roberts, for marketing assistance.

To Scott Davis, who models the positive attitude.

And most prominently for Peter who is who he is: a luminous being, a sage, a friend, an inspiration and model for me.

How to Read this Book

The two volumes of this book have been designed to help you quickly and easily find whatever topic you are interested in or need information about. Are you having problems with illness? Turn to "Healing Yourself," or "What Causes Accidents and Illnesses." Do you need help with finances? Then read "Creating Wealth," or "The Way to Success."

You can also read the book from front to back, cover to cover, or you can just read the questions and answers. It is the type of book that invites you to open it at random and enjoy whatever gem of wisdom you encounter. The grouping of paragraphs under short subsections lends itself to this usage, making it fun and easy to use in this way.

Peter recommends reading inspirational material before going to bed at night. The subsections in each chapter, as well as the question and answer format make it easy to pick up the book, read a little, and put it down before retiring, or anytime you have a few moments to spare.

Every effort has been made to make this information as clear and accessible as possible given its esoteric nature. To avoid the unwieldiness of using "he or she" and "himself or herself" in each case concerning an individual, the pronouns have been used alternately.

If you read this book with an open heart and mind (and put your prejudices aside even if you may sometimes disagree with what is said), you may find that you catch a glimpse of the unknown, a glimpse into the vastness of possibility that is your birthright.

Volume One of *The Moth Comes to the Flame* contains chapters pertaining to Life, Self, Relationships and Emotions. Taken together, both volumes form a continuum, beginning with Life and touching on all aspects of the spiritual journey until ending with a chapter on Enlightenment.

- John Roberts

A Note About the Questions and Answers

John, from my perspective, every question is just asking for the direction home. There is only one answer to every question, but many questions there are, all placed on top of each other. It is much like an old, run-down house. So, please bear with me as I begin to rip off the roof and tear down the walls and sweep away the ghosts. With all this debris and carnage littering the site, be patient with me, and you will see with eyes of surprise the foundation upon which it all rests. I promise not to abandon you, but to build you up soundly, to inspire and encourage you. Not with false hopes, promises and flimsy premises, but on solid ground, with a firm foundation. Upon the cornerstone of consciousness a new trust will arise, a new confidence and a certainty of soul! Your questions may not be answered in the conventional manner, but in a way that hopefully will lead them to dissolve.

- Peter

The wheel eternal in its relentless roll, crushes all. The spokes, like people, point first to this and then to that, to 10,000 objects which are never really seen. The tears of the sage wash the dust from the 10,000 illusions. The tears of the sage flow from the empty hub upon which the universe revolves. The sage, the seer, scopes the infinite vistas of the unspeakable realm and trembles... for the tears are for you.

- Peter

Mind

Are You Aware and Conscious?

The Secret of the Touchstone

Here is a story as old as time: When the great library in ancient Alexandria was burned, only a few writings survived. One was a velvet-covered book of parchment, and in it was the story of the "Secret of the Touchstone." As the story goes, there was a magical stone, warm to the touch, that lay on a rock-strewn beach along the Black Sea. Whoever found the touchstone could turn base metals into gold and have any wish granted.

In Varna, off the coast of Bulgaria on the Black Sea, a man looked endlessly for the magical touchstone. As the days went by he would pick up a stone and throw it into the sea, pick up another stone and throw it into the sea and so on and so on. One day he picked up a stone and threw it into the sea — and realized too late that it had been the magic touchstone!

See What Is Right Before You

See what is right before you with clarity; don't throw it away. Appreciate and behold that which has real value and that which enriches your life right now. In spite of all the searching, you toss away opportunities every day. Practice awareness — it is your safeguard. Be aware instead of habitual. Change your patterns and your daily routines if you tend to run through them unconsciously.

There is a biblical quote, "Do not forsake the day of little things." Do not neglect the little things in your life. Be aware. Be conscious. Look, watch and listen. You attend to the details of life effortlessly when you are more conscious.

Awareness Comes Before Consciousness

We must first practice awareness of the world around us. Then, as we focus our concentration, we become more conscious, and the intensity of consciousness allows us to see the real nature of things. When conscious, we can remember and perceive things at a much deeper level than those who only see surface appearances.

To be happy, you must be able to perceive reality. To be focused, practice doing one thing at a time and doing it extremely well. Make your meditation active and alive in the moment. Walk, talk, sit and move consciously. Be aware of how you feel, how you breathe, and how you gesture.

Awareness Allows Us to See Cause and Effect

To reason, to be able to think with clarity and understand the laws of cause and effect and see their outworking in one's life, is a joy indeed. Pain and suffering in one's life is an indication that one has not been able to choose wisely and truly understand the working of cause and effect in life. Whatever the thought or activity is, it brings either blessings or curses, and only in the full light of consciousness can one choose rightly.

The Ten Commandments Shouldn't Be Needed

For people who are conscious, laws such as the Ten Commandments are not needed. It is rather elementary that someone should have to tell you, "Don't kill," or, "Don't steal."

Consciousness Is the Divine Spark of Life that Lights Your World

Hold on your screen of consciousness one thought at a time. Practice being where you are. You are here, in the moment, exuberantly alive. This truth is obvious if you are not mentally everywhere else.

Consciousness is the divine spark of life that makes it all glow. Our conscious thoughts are living things — they create our reality. There is an intimate connection between our thoughts, which become our prayers and dreams, and our reality. When we vividly focus on our faculty of consciousness, we in essence blow on a spark and fan its flames into a bright light.

The divine spark is found in the most unusual places. What is sparking around us? The energy behind our sparks hovers around us electromagnetically and becomes solidified into form. We make our dreams reality by working with universal laws, making them our own.

When you imagine something, the body responds to that image. When you imagine some physical feat, the body reacts. You can imagine, for instance, that you are running, and you will notice very subtle muscular contractions in your legs. It is the mind's images that control the physical body. Images solidify and become our reality. Be careful: What you see is what you get!

Concentration Leads to Meditation Which Leads to Super-Consciousness

The brain is a three-pound, pink and gray mass with 20 billion nerve endings. What allows the brain to do what it does? It is the mind that causes the brain to create vivid, lifelike, three-dimensional images and trigger a complex array of neurochemicals that allows us to project the outside world inside our heads.

The Moth Comes to the Flame

The brain is the physical offspring of the mind. The mind is powered by consciousness and affects the brain. It is the mind that gives the instructions to the body; the mind programs the body.

Using the brain requires 20 percent of the body's energy, so when we concentrate, we must call on our internal energy reserves which requires conscious effort. That is why so few appear able to unravel life's problems. To consciously suspend thought requires even more energy but, once accomplished, results in a greater return of energy.

Practice in using what's between our ears develops the ability to focus first on our thoughts, then on the moment of time between the thoughts. You can develop this ability by the practice of concentrating on one thing at a time. This concentration will lead to meditation, which in turn leads to heightened states of consciousness.

One of the best ways to learn to concentrate is to practice any of the methods of "listening to your breath." It is the breath that connects the mind to the body.

The Clearer Your Screen of Consciousness, the More Immediately Your Reality Is Created

The sharper your ability to image, the quicker your reality manifests. High achievers see things vividly in their minds. A luminous being visualizes in animated sensory detail. Without vivid images, we cannot attend to the greatness of life.

Take Charge of Your Reality

To take charge of your reality you must become more conscious. Consciousness is a powerful tool. When you are very conscious, you do not need to use an alarm clock or a ruler; your internal conscious awareness will give you the correct time and measurements.

(You should see Peter doing carpentry work, or experience his uncanny perception of time and distance.)

The More You Know, the Odder You Become

We must master the physical realm first. We are conscious to the degree that we perceive that which is. The more you perceive, the odder (unusual) you are. And, the odder you are, the more ecstasy you have.

"The Watcher" Is Our Consciousness

When we develop focused awareness, we evolve in our consciousness. What you see on the inside is what you get on the outside. Check on the inside to see that everything is in order. If it is not, the outside will be in disarray. Ask who is the one seeing, who is this that is watching? When consciousness becomes aware of itself it is called enlightenment, or as Peter would say, "The moth does more than flirt with the flame."

*Everyone is free to be unconscious,
but not free to avoid the consequences
of this unconsciousness.*

QUESTIONS AND ANSWERS

In this chapter and on other occasions you have made what some might feel are critical comments about the Ten Commandments. Would you like to clarify?

My comments are no more critical than those recorded and attributed to Jesus. Jesus said he came not to destroy the Mosaic Law Code but to be the fulfillment of it. He said that all the thousands of years of written laws and regulations (that, by the way, not one person in Israel could even follow) could be summed up in this: "Love one another as I have loved you, and love God with your whole heart, mind and strength." He was an overshadowing example of the development of a perfect man, a man who needed no laws of social or religious convention or invention, a man whose spiritual experience transcended law. Jesus was a man who climbed to the summit of human excellence, a man who was the epitome of high ideals, love, wisdom and strength.

How can Jesus ever be compared to a bunch of animalistic savages lost in a desert? Savage to the point that they need to be given strict laws not to murder each other or rape another's wife or steal, and so on. Would you give such a law to intelligent people? Of course not! Their hearts, minds, awareness and conscience would never allow them to behave in such a decadent, debased and savage manner.

The unspoken, unwritten law of love that swells the human heart and gives it wings to fly to the Father, that and that alone is what one lives by, for "God is Love." Carved in granite or impressed in gold, these impostors can never replace the law of love written in our hearts. To give man another law is to insult and slander the Christ in our hearts.

When we are very young, our conscience is alive and fresh by virtue of an innocent consciousness, much like a sharply pointed triangle. Imagine this triangle spinning in our heart every time we violate the law of love. Over countless revolutions of the triangle, the once-pointed tips that used to cause such pain are now round and smooth and the heart cave calloused with scar tissue. No longer do we hearken to the heart's cries for solace. No longer do we feel our heart's pain. Now this dangerous creature who has lost both heart and conscience must have the prison bars of law to protect us from his evil desires. To him give the Ten Commandments, and the world will be protected for a brief moment longer.

You made the statement, "The moth does more than flirt with the flame." Would you care to elaborate?

On the surface it appears the moth is the seeker and the sage is the flame. When the seeker is sincere, the flame is compelling — so compelling, so alluring, that the seeker's single-minded focus is only on eliminating any distance between himself and the very source of illumination. As gas merges with air and salt with water, the moth is driven by this irresistible force into the flame. Now the moth is consumed by the fire, and both the moth and his world have disappeared.

When the seeker first comes close to the sage he feels the heat. Many of his cherished assumptions, opinions and beliefs go up in flames as they cannot bear the fire of inspection. At this stage the seeker feels both free and frightened, but now with less weighing him down, he comes yet closer. So close, in fact, that everything the seeker thought to be his identity is burned and gone. Now that all has disappeared, the seeker becomes the sage.

Now for the last part of the divine drama. In truth there is no seeker and there is no sage. There is only consciousness seeking to know itself. The soul is the seed and this earth, the soil. The seed becomes the seeker and the world becomes the teacher. When the seeker sees the world as teacher, the moth has flirted with the flame. When the seeker becomes the world, the moth is swallowed by the light.

When the seeker does more than flirt with the flame, both seeker and sage cease to be and consciousness has become aware of itself.

Mind: Are You Aware and Conscious?

That's beautiful, but it seems paradoxical. Can you tell us more about how consciousness can be aware of itself?

Certainly, if you can drop the question! That is why the ancients gave seekers the symbol of the snake swallowing its tail. It's just as simple as the implicate and explicate order of quantum physics. Again I say, you must drop the question to know the answer.

Developing Your Intuition

**Intuition Is a Matter of
Being Highly Conscious**

Develop your ordinary sensory perception, and you'll be amazed at your increased extrasensory perception. The ESP will fill in the blanks between your observations — so open your eyes and ears!

We can only trust our intuition to the degree that we are confident with our ordinary sensory perception. We have to get OSP, ordinary sensory perception, before we get ESP, extraordinary sensory perception. If you have OSP, most people will think you have ESP because so few have the ability to perceive the world accurately with their senses.

Intuition Is the Teacher Within

Intuition is the teacher within you. When you listen carefully to the call within, it is always real. Do not color it with self depreciation. You come to know that your intuition is right based upon thousands of past correct conclusions. Every time you have a lightning flash of reason, it's intuition, and it gets better. The "in tutor" (intuition) inside you knows what is right and what is not.

At higher levels of being, our thoughts become very powerful, immediately creating consequences. When you think of someone and the phone rings, or someone receives a gift from you and you know right when she receives and opens it, it is your higher knowing at work.

Our intuition helps us know about people, even new individuals we meet. When you meet someone new who reminds you of two people you already know, do a cross-check and you'll realize that — since function follows form — they will all have similarities. The new person will be somewhat similar to a cross between the two people you already know. You'll be amazed at the similarities. From this thread you can gently pull all types of information about this person from the hidden realm of your intuition.

There is a Doorway to Intuition

You can use the early morning and late evening hours to be very relaxed and gain insights that are beneficial. Just let go and relax. In that state between consciousness and sleep, there is a doorway to a different dimension. This is a space where insights and observations can be very clear, concise and accurate. Just lie there and practice witnessing everything around you. At these times there are powerful energies that abound. You'll learn a lot about yourself, for you are more open to intuitive flashes.

Intuition Is a Lightning Bolt of Reason

Intuition is information, or knowledge, based on countless correct conclusions stored in the subconscious. Develop clarity of intuition and you will find it precisely on target. The sudden realization that you "know" is intuition. It is lightning-bolt reasoning on a subconscious level.

Intuition is nourished when you can see the cause and effect relationships everywhere. The world is a fascinating story to be "read" when you are aware enough to see. Unconditioned young children often have phenomenal intuition and experiences. Frequently they will see the "colored lights" (auras) around people, but are often conditioned not to speak of them or believe their own eyes. Eventually, they lose the ability to see the colors and the magic has died.

Be acutely focused, acutely aware.

QUESTIONS AND ANSWERS

Okay, Peter. In *The Fruit of Your Thoughts,* I tell the story of how you told me exactly where to find the photo for the cover of the book and what it would look like. You even told me that the photo was taken in "a golden wheat field just north of McCall, Idaho." Even though you haven't been to Idaho since the 1940s, you were right! So how did you use your intuition to divine that?

About the photograph, John, I need no wings to get there, and I need no eyes in order to see.

I have experienced that to be true with you, Peter. I have another question: Do you see the auras around people as is described in this chapter?

Seeing auras doesn't make one a high spiritual being. I can teach anyone to see the aura of the physical body in less than five minutes' time. It is as simple as seeing heat radiation emanating from a hot stove.

If you focus your eyes in a rather detached manner, just as the mind is detached in meditation, you will begin to see an amazing display. But you must have "young" eyes. By that I mean eyes full of innocence and wonder. Old eyes are vapid from years of being sated, satiated, and filled beyond capacity with the frivolous and mundane. Old eyes are a result of a lifetime spent in the pursuit of new sensations and pleasures. Young eyes are curious, bright and free of judgment. This childlike sense of awe is what enables one to see beyond the physical. You do not see the spiritual aura with physical eyes. The only thing seen with the physical eyes are the very subtle colors associated with the body's energy field.

There are countless books on the market about auras. Many of them are just holy cow dung. Some mention stories about people whose auras are so bright that you could read a newspaper in a dark room by their light. Personally, well, let's say that's cute. A blind man can read a newspaper in a dark room if he has learned to see with his spiritual eyes. Spiritual luminescence is not physical and thus not seen with physical eyes. This is why the scriptures refer to seeing with the single eye. The eye symbolizes spiritual sight. And it's only through this kind of seeing that one would be able to see a Jesus, or a Buddha.

The fool who can't even find his glasses because they are hidden on his face is now suddenly supposed to see the messiah coming on a cloud? By the way, the word messiah is parousia *in Greek. That means a "presence." It is stated that Christ's return would be in the same manner as was his departure, unnoticed, private and invisible to the crude, insensitive and spiritually blind. This energy field, or invisible presence, is here now to be seen with spiritual eyes alone. It is a luminous pool of spiritual light that one may be immersed in and cleansed of karma. And it is true that Jesus said, "I will be with you always." How could there be a coming or, for that matter, a going away? He has prepared a place for us by entering nirvana, and when we enter the emptiness of that sacred heart cave, we will be swallowed by its light.*

Dreams

Most Dreams Are Just Mental Garbage Coming Out

Dreams can be overlooked because they are only mental garbage, just as our stool is physical garbage. Dreams are indicators of cleansings or an increase in toxins that are warnings of physical disease. It is helpful to remember our dreams, even the nightmares, so that we can clear them out. Toxins thrown into the blood, which flows through the brain, create certain images.

"Mental diverticulitis" is when an unexpected release of stored mental concepts come out in the form of dreams. Sometimes taking extra supplements or increasing aerobic exercise will create more dreams when either is initially started. They trigger the release of new toxic chemical flows.

The same happens during fasting. During long fasts done for religious reasons, many folks have reported beautiful visions. Of course, it depends on your upbringing as to whether you see Jesus or Krishna. When the brain's protein levels reach low stores, hallucinations occur. Consider the accounts of people shipwrecked for long periods of time or lost in the desert.

Dreaming Allows You to Get Rid of Toxicity

If your nights are restless from dreams, work toward becoming physically cleaner, mentally clearer and less distressed during your day. When your days are filled with life-affirming and not life-negating ideas, you will feel good. The dreams will be better as well. If there are destructive experiences during the day, you will need to perform a mental fast, sometimes by a silent retreat, so that your dreams can calm down.

Precognitive Dreams

Sometimes there are precognitive-type dreams where information comes to you in the night.

These are intuitive hunches that, when perfectly clear, can be helpful.

Spiritual Dreams and Hallucinations — Are They the Same?

Insane and even many so-called sane people cannot differentiate between night dreams and daydreams. The psychotic person may often reach a state where they can't differentiate between the awake state and the dream state. In other words, they are dreaming of being awake and living and moving within that dream while asleep. Just consider your state of functioning if, while at your place of employment, you suddenly dreamt you were elsewhere or your boss suddenly changed into another person. You can see the obvious difficulties. Polluted bodies produce polluted minds which lead to insanity, and the polluted mind gives birth to a polluted body as well.

Distrust all dreams.

QUESTIONS AND ANSWERS

This last statement, "distrust all dreams" is going to cause quite a stir amongst many of our readers. What are you saying?

John, if we go into a darkened movie house, sit down comfortably and start watching the film being projected on the screen, if the story is captivating, isn't it odd how quickly we become engrossed and forget ourselves? Not much difference between that movie and the movies we play in our heads that we call dreams or daydreams. We still forget ourselves. So, here you are watching this interesting movie in the theater and suddenly the lights go on. What happened to the screen? You may call that enlightenment, though this is a very gross analogy. The mind is like film, composed of isolated stills of memories, facts, thoughts, and abstractions that are like layers of snapshots in the film. This film is not just your individual mind, but a universal mind. It is more like a holographic plate that produces three-dimensional, nonexistent images when the laser light is penetrating the film plate at a certain angle. Change the angle, you change the scene.

In a sense you choose the movie of your life. Quantum physics refers to an implicate order and an explicate order. The implicate is similar to an invisible film plate. A film plate that is "enfolded," unseen. The explicate is the manifested or "unfolded" world, or perhaps I should say, dream. It is the light of consciousness penetrating the film that produces the world. What do you see when you are unconscious? What do you see when deeply engrossed in a daydream? Only in perfect, unadulterated consciousness do you see reality. When the lights go on, only then can you see what is really there. The hypnotic effect of the dream is gone, and you have become awakened. Remember, all dreams oppose reality.

Then, why do we dream?

To simply process mental images we do not know what to do with. Dreams are an attempt to make sense and order out of abstractions. Mental food or physical food is processed in the same manner, excretion, but do you stick your head down into the toilet and say, "Gee, was it corn or taters I ate the other day?" Do you sit down there and start divining the floating pieces of stool as if they were tea leaves in a cup? Well, I suppose some might....

What if you did notice that the stool was bloody, black, or resembled a corn-like material, or perhaps fuzz balls with long black streamers, or what looked like gelatin capsules? These can be indications of everything from cancer to diverticulitis. So what do you do now? You stop putting into your body the foods that cause these symptoms. You need but notice it just once and get busy clearing up the problem.

Dreams are symptoms of mental gluttony, mental constipation. As soon as you clean out your system with the purgative of awareness and the light of consciousness, they will begin to cease and your mental health will improve.

Since we use our physical bodies to process the foods we eat, the cleaner the food, the quicker it exits and the less the residue. Since we use our mental bodies to process the thoughts we think, the cleaner, the more accurate the thought, the less the mental burden, and yes, the less the dream time in processing it out of the system.

The issue still remains, how long do you want to sleep and dream before you awaken to reality? All dreams are delusion, only consciousness can reveal reality.

The Need for Clarity

How Stubborn Are You?

A battleship was heading on a straight course when a young seaman in charge saw a light ahead. He radioed and told the other ship to go 20 degrees to the right, but it did not change course. He repeated his request, but the other ship refused to move.

Finally the captain came to the helm and took the radio and told the other light to go 20 degrees to the right. From the other radio came the response, "You go twenty degrees right." The captain became agitated and stated, "I am a captain, go 20 degrees to the right." The radio signal came back, "I am a seaman 2nd class, you go 20 degrees to the right."

The Moth Comes to the Flame

The captain by now was furious and stated, "I am a battleship. I demand you go 20 degrees to the right."

And the radio signal came back, "I am a lighthouse. You go 20 degrees to the right."

* * *

This story illustrates how, in our stubborn minds, we see things our way rather than looking at reality as it is. Quite frankly, when our illusions crash into reality, we will suddenly see the light. How stubborn are you?

Things are never exactly as they appear unless you can see perfectly. Clarity is a necessity. Clear thought leads to clear seeing which leads to greater levels of consciousness. Greater levels of consciousness lead to super-consciousness which leads to total aliveness. When such vibrancy exists, you can't even explain how the grass appears fluorescent to you, while others barely see the grass. Everything is more vibrant, more real and more luminous.

When You See with Clarity, You Are Free

You don't have to work for enlightenment. Just stop resisting and fighting against life. Then you can be ordinary for the first time. Then you are content just to be yourself, your essential essence. When you forget about it, you'll be shocked at how fast you discover your enlightenment.

See what is right before you with clarity; don't throw away the grand opportunity. Appreciate and behold that which can unveil itself as reality, that which is so rich and is there before you right now.

It takes long periods of honesty for clarity and vision to develop. One must have clarity before intentions can be empowered. Good intentions are not enough; consciousness is needed.

Life Is About Not Getting Blinded by the Fog

In 1952, Florence Chadwick was swimming from Catalina Island to the California coast, a distance of 21 miles. Through bone-numbing cold, fog, and shark-infested waters she swam 15 hours.

Florence wanted to give up but was coaxed on by her mother and others in an accompanying boat. But at last, exhausted, she crawled into the boat.

Later, Florence discovered she had been only a mile from shore — but the fog had kept her from seeing how close she was to reaching her goal. After this experience, Florence stated she would never give up again.

Florence could not see through the fog. We, too, have a fog that doesn't let us see our goal. The fog is the thousand different opinions we hold and countless little subconscious urges of things not good for you. Say "Peace, be still" to the urges, opinions and suggestions that crowd your head. Learn to quiet the mind, and listen to your in-tutor (intuition). When you have done so, a beautiful stillness and calm will descend upon you. Keep your eyes on the prize, hold high ideals and visions, and you will never be blinded by the fog.

Clairvoyance Means Clear Sight

Clear sight is seeing through a clarified aura with no static energy or fog banks to block the light.

Mind: The Need for Clarity

Listening and hearing are different. When the heart and mind are combined, we listen. When we start developing our intuition and reason, the fog begins to lift. Be quiet and observe what you are thinking. Allow only one thought at a time. Do one activity at a time with full concentration and awareness. Our thoughts are akin to puffy white clouds against a clear blue sky. We can have puffy thoughts or a clear blue consciousness.

The secret of life is to become watchful and meditative. How can we experience authentic meditation? Practice being alert and aware in all things. Are you focused and attentive to what is going on around you? It takes focus, and at first it can be arduous and tiring, much like learning to play a musical instrument, but later it becomes effortless and enjoyable.

Develop Clarity with Practice

You develop clarity by practice. Be diligent in your practice; the value is in the effort involved. It is the journey up the mountain that makes each step a new vision and the mountaintop worthwhile. The journey is as much the goal as the peak.

How Shall I Live Today?

The key is in this moment, now. How do you want to live it? Ask yourself, "How can I have a blissful, luminous life now?" To be truly effective in life you must question things.

Most people live lives in the hazy realm of "guessology," never taking time to think on their own and ask vital, perceptive questions.

Four questions to ask are:
1. What is it?
2. Where did it come from?
3. How do I know it?
4. What should I do about it?

To fully live we must be fully conscious. Ask what it is, where it came from, how you know it, and what you should do about it. If you don't know what it is and can't find out, forget it. Always consider how you can verify a thought, belief or physical event, and then decide what you should do about it on the basis of the above questions.

Allow only one thought at a time.

QUESTIONS AND ANSWERS

How do you arrive at such clarity? You speak for days without a single note, an unheard of accomplishment. You quote Indian scriptures in Sanskrit, and chapter and verse from the Bible and other esoteric texts. You speak so extensively on medical issues that the doctors in the audience think you just graduated from medical school. You dazzle the history teachers, and when you talk physics, you are a scientist. How did you develop such incredible skills? And, all of this with *no* formal education — that baffles the professors who sit in your audience as well as everyone else.

Okay, let's look at the issue of clarity. Have you ever been introduced to a stranger one minute and then forgotten his name the next? So often names are just meaningless conglomerations of sound. It's not that we have forgotten the name, it's that we never heard it in the first place. Why? Mostly because we didn't think it important enough to remember. We may have reasoned, "Why put forth this mental effort to remember when I'll probably never meet this person again?" Or, "So what if I don't remember? This person is not important." But when we take the position that every little thing is important, that everything is a sign, an indicator, a portent or an omen, we pay more attention. When we give our undivided attention to anything, we are exercising a mental faculty called "original awareness." In order to have original awareness, we must not allow competing thoughts to distract and drug our clarity. Laser-like focus and concentration on one thing at a time is called for.

The reason I can speak for days on end without notes on any topic is that I only have one thought at a time. My mental book is opened to one page with only one thought on it. So, it is very effortless for me to relate what I have before me. I simply tell you what I see and turn the page. Since each page is connected to the next, I always know where I am going and where I have been. This way I am able to repeat what I said two hours before if asked but do not repeat myself from two hours earlier because I "forgot" what I said.

Mind: The Need for Clarity

Where does the knowledge come from?

First of all, it's written everywhere. Pull on the string of secular knowledge and sources appear as easily in your head as if you just pulled up someone's web page. But, there is more. I have acute knowledge of my own experience and that, more importantly, is what is so easy to express. The difficult part is for you to understand what I am really saying and for me to help you to understand. The easy part is to dazzle you with mental prowess. Any fool can do that.

Do you speed read?

If you know eternity, what's the purpose? Though I must admit it only took a few minutes to read Evelyn Wood's book on speed reading, my first reading of the Bible *took two years; my first reading of the* Bhagavad Gita *took two years. My second reading of them took much longer. And similarly with countless other ancient texts, the* Dhammapada, *the* Tao Te Ching, *the* Yoga Sutras of Patanjali *and so on.*

You see John, I don't grab grub or eat at fast food restaurants. I have learned to chew thoroughly and digest what I feel is worthy of consumption. Do you speed read poetry? Of course you don't. Does one gulp down, like a hungry dog, a book that expresses a lifetime of experience, or one that is filled with the eternal wisdom of the ages? That person is no more than a hungry, hairless ape. Music is music because of the spaces between the notes, otherwise it would just be noise. Clarity is the space that allows the notes to become music.

May the music of your silent spaces fill the world with song.

The Power of Thought

**Imagery Creates a Magnetic
Force Field of Attraction**

The images we hold are so powerful that if we're not conscious of their results in our lives, we could find ourselves subscribing to fate or luck instead of deliberate design.

Our entire bodies are a system of memory. When we think, electrical impulses emanate out from us and magnetize similar thoughts and conditions to return to us. This means that your word is your magic wand. It won't fail to get the desired results. The more emotionally-charged and vivid your words and images, the more rapidly they manifest. "I can do this thing," is a statement of power that you can align with.

Our intentions either scatter the forces, making them impotent, or create what we want which is the mirror image of our real thoughts. Be focused. Our conscious thoughts are living things — they create our reality. There is an intimate connection between our thoughts and that which becomes our reality. When we vividly imagine, focus and concentrate on a certain attainment, that imagery will grow from a tiny spark into a large flame of reality and manifestation.

There is a saying regarding the laws of attraction: If you put a decoy on the lake, the real ducks will come. When you understand what initiates a cause, you'll begin to get glimpses of reality. Hold "possibility" thoughts of a high vibratory nature — with great positiveness and energy — and you will begin to create greatness in your life.

What You Focus on Expands

What you focus on expands. If you have fearful thoughts, you will have fearful circumstances. Beautiful thoughts lead to beautiful circumstances. You initiate the causes to get the beautiful effects. You get whatever you want. See it in sensory detail, and it's soon to be accomplished. Like a snapshot, take it and forget it until it's developed. You just did your part, and now the universal law will work its part. If you can visualize a black bear with a yellow party hat, stop and consider how you created this image. Not knowing how you formed an image with sensory detail in your head is not a problem, but the fact that you had this wonderful ability to create should encourage you to create beauty all around you. Visualization is that simple.

We have the infinite power to choose. It's incredible to believe we don't. Problems come because we choose the wrong thoughts. There is no freedom possible if you hold tenaciously to the belief that you have no control over your thoughts, that they just happen to you. They do not just happen. You were taught certain limiting beliefs, and you have embraced them for so long that you do not know you have the choice to leave enslavement.

Strong and Happy Thoughts Heal the Body

The brain experiences words as sound vibrations, and when those words are spoken with emotion, added power is the effect. Your words are an expression of the mental energy of your mind. Sounds and thoughts vibrate; they have a resonance like music. Brain wave patterns are affected by your thoughts and words.

Every word has a vibration, and these words vibrate much the same in many languages. As an example, the word "good" produces the same vibration no matter if it's said in Bulgarian or Finnish. Pleasant thoughts create biomagnetic messages in the brain which are, in turn, sent to our immune system, other glands, and nerve plexuses throughout the body. We produce endorphins that heal our body and give us that overall feeling of well-being.

Our health is a direct result of our pattern of thinking and speaking. When there have been long periods of mental abuse, the body becomes shell-shocked. Too often we overtax the neurophysical system. Illness and disease are disasters of disruption to an otherwise healthy state of being. They simply have been created in the mind by our thoughts. Long-harbored confusion and non-peaceful thinking wear our system down.

Mind: The Power of Thought

Thoughts bring security and peacefulness to the body if they are good, and confusion to the body when they are toxic. Whenever you imagine something, your body responds to that image. When one imagines some physical feat, the body reacts. It is the mind's images that control the physical body. Images solidify. Heaven and hell, life and death, are just a thought apart. Thoughts can bring serenity or confusion.

Every thought of limitation is an unconscious thought of "I can't," which is really an "I won't." We create ourselves anew every moment, with every thought. Sick individuals often run away from facing their responsibilities, and they lose sight of their purpose, thus frustration and despair give birth to illness.

The power of your thoughts can heal you or kill you. As an example, don't talk about how old, how fat, how skinny or how sick you are because your body is likely to hear you and manifest your imagination. What you are thinking can change the state of your health so quickly it can even melt cancer tumors like snow balls on a hot stove. If you vividly and emotionally imagine something, you will create it.

You cannot control your body if you cannot control your thoughts. Your life span goes way down if you believe you're not in control of your mind and body. The future is created by thoughts in the moment, and these seed thoughts grow your future. When you have illuminated thoughts in the moment, life is so beautiful that one's cup runneth over and no more can be added.

Learn to Take the Bad Things in Life and Readjust Them

It is our sense of adaptability that builds and gives us a positive and fruitful future. Drop all old limitation thinking. You need not hold withering and debilitating thoughts even if they were taught to you as a child. Child researchers say that up to the age of seven children cannot tell the truth from a lie. When a child is taught limitation thinking such as, "You'll get hurt if you try that," or "You're too small," "too young," "too frail," or they hear "Let father do it for you," and so on, they believe it. Some lies get told throughout lifetimes and even go back to the start of time, and thus, they are deeply embedded into our genes. If you experienced some of these lies, you must unlearn them. Adjust what life gave you and make it work for you by focusing on the seed of positive growth and positive lessons.

Life is risky. So what's new? Don't be a wallflower, go dance the dance of life. Be a gambler. Gamble for the good life — for that which makes you become more. You don't have to live like the majority of people on this planet. Gamble on the fact that the lies you heard when young can be overcome. Gamble on living life luminously and joyously.

You Are Only Limited by Your Beliefs

There is nothing you cannot do unless you believe you cannot do it. What is it you really desire, think about and concentrate upon? Focus on that one thing and it will expand, reveal and manifest itself. Consider how the scientist focuses on one thing with great mental intensity and sooner or later a breakthrough takes place because he refuses to be distracted.

You can hold one-pointed focus even while you are aware of all of the happenings along the periphery. There are also breath control techniques that build unbelievable degrees of laser-like concentration, because the breath is the connection between mind and body

Not Thinking Can Get Us Into a Lot of Trouble

Animals think in terms of subsistence for today: for food, survival and pleasure. They do not consider or philosophize about eternity; only man does that. Plants acquire life through the light of the sun. They reach toward the sun which is good for them. Plants and animals cannot work consciously against their own survival, but people can because they have the freedom to contemplate countless options on how to live. Animals and plants are already preprogrammed, but we have an option to be more than our programming. We have the ability to work toward or against our own best interest. Working toward our best interest requires clear thinking. Don't think and trouble can arrive quicker than a blink of an eye.

Many individuals subconsciously work to sabotage their lives. Some even want to leave the earth to get a fresh start because they don't recognize in their unreasoning moods that they have the right to happiness here and now. They do not realize that the application of energy is good and provides greater comfort and joy in the life before us.

It takes clear thinking to have an effective and purposeful direction. You experience great fulfillment when you take control of your reality and create an artistically beautiful life. There was once an outrageous bumper sticker that read, "Living Well Is the Best Revenge."

When You Know Yourself, You Start to Know Others as Well

A focused mind can only exist when we get rid of the clouds of distracting thoughts and our obsessions with pleasure, both of which arise from the mental weakness of being unable to resist immediate gratification. If we would learn how to think rationally, we would not need armies, politicians, preachers or prisons. Teachers would then share their skill levels so effectively that the job of the teacher would be to have no students. The teacher's role is to dispel the darkness and guide others into successful living and a fulfilling life of satisfying and worthwhile accomplishments.

When you find a master teacher, he will know what you are thinking and why. He does not tell us what to do but may ask if we've thought of looking at something this way or that way. Since electrical charges travel through the ethers and thoughts are electro-magnetic, a teacher can hold loving thoughts and affect the person they are thinking of from any distance. We are all teachers to a degree and can affect healing by having concentrated loving thoughts, rather than fearful, judgmental thoughts.

Your Mind Is More Powerful Than You Imagined

What you perceive about yourself is always true because you make it true in time. Do not hold to dark thoughts because they are the registered trauma of every cell in your body. Watch that you only hold positive thoughts about yourself, and you will discover there is an energy inside that always takes care of you. When you have discovered that, you will realize you will always come out safe.

Whatever You Want, Wants You

Thoughts go out and bring back to you what you ask for based on what you hold in your mind. Every thought is a prayer, so watch out what you program yourself for. Once your visions are keyed onto a target they may zig-zag but once beamed in on your target of what you want in your life — no matter how elusive it seems and no matter how many twists and turns it takes — the goal will be hit.

You'll recognize that thoughts retrieve themselves. Thoughts are like living entities that go out and do your bidding. The more powerful your thoughts the more you reel your goals in. Miracles are just unexplained universal laws. The more you understand the construct of their workings the more focused and more immediate the creation.

Every Thought Creates an Effect

Emotions in action follow every thought. There is also something behind the thought. When you discover this energy behind the thought, you'll get a sense of what we really are. Could it be light in slow motion? When the vibration flows, the material manifests. You could perhaps call it the revelation of God in human form.

Do Not Be Smothered by Other People's Opinions

Sometimes we are smothered by our thoughts. Most people's minds are made up of nothing else but other people's opinions. The reason we experience difficulty being around certain people is that their thought patterns are not electromagnetically compatible with ours. If we don't mentally speak the same language, there is a gap in communication. Without communication there can be no harmony, and without harmony there can be no peace.

Empty Yourself of the Useless So That You May Be Filled with the Valuable

There is a story of a Zen master who kept pouring tea even after the cup was full. The guest witnessing this asked what he was doing. The Master said, "Yes, it's just like your mind. Like the cup, your mind is full and running over. Go empty yourself and then come back, and I will fill it with something else."

What is the best way to remove the veil of illusion or *maya*? Do all you can to clear the head that is filled with useless thoughts, clutter, chatter and illusions. A head full of clutter is like a car driving with no one steering. It cannot be directed for there are too many conflicting messages.

The Mind Is Under Your Control

When we can think clearly, rationally and consciously, there will be no competition with conflicting thoughts and ideas. The brain is controlled by the mind, but we are not accustomed to controlling our minds and, thus, the difficulty. Our thoughts are often self-fulfilling prophecies.

If our attitude is good, the results are good. A poor attitude leads to poor results. A fair attitude results in fair outcomes. Our mental expectations form our attitudes. Remember, expectations are formed by thoughts.

Take out the useless garbage from your mind. It's like cleaning out your computer's hard disk. The process is like tossing out the useless old files or cleaning old clothes out of your closet. It is your belief that you cannot take control of your mind that stops you.

Your memory will improve when you get rid of the clutter. Much of memory is stored as words which are identified as pictures. Keep that which has relevance and value in living a beautiful life. The secret to miracles happening in your life is to think in a concentrated way and with purpose. Get the crowd out of your head. Discipline yourself to have one thought at a time.

Time moves like a train, but life is in the moment.

Think Without Distraction

A sage was once asked the secret to his happiness. He said, "When I walk, I walk; when I sit, I sit; when I draw water from the well, I draw water from the well." He learned one-pointed focus in the present moment. So when we are painting, playing music or participating in a recreational event, we, also, can do just that.

The Positive Power Surge

The power of intention is also the energy of a motivating spirit. With the right focused intention, we can experience incredible power surges that give us an exhilarating boost. You may feel an unusual energy, like an electrical surge through your nervous system, when sitting quietly in meditation or when incredibly focused on a specific activity. The surge may come with perfect stillness. Whenever it comes, simply allow it.

The surge only comes when we are not "busy" up in the head. The ability to think things over one at a time and focus like a laser helps to prepare us. It is when we are without thought and just sitting still that an experience, a surge of overwhelming peace, floods our being.

There are only two kinds of thoughts:
Life-affirming or life-negating,
blossoming thoughts or withering thoughts.

We Have a Responsibility Toward Excellence

All minds emit electromagnetic forces. When we seek excellence, our little light has great power and scatters the darkness. Light always has power. Be a powerful, light-generating person with thoughts of excellence. Become like a warm fire on a dark, cold night. People who are tired of shivering in the cold will be drawn by your warmth. People who would like to fan the flames of their own excellence will seek your company.

Light one candle and it will scatter the darkness. Be that candle.

We Radiate Electromagnetic Fields

The brain is a cognitive tool that operates on vibrations. We radiate electromagnetic fields when we think. When you turn up your electromagnetic voltage, you will alter your reality. Look at the results in your life. If a farmer plants seeds and nothing good comes as a result — if weeds come instead of produce — the farmer changes the seed next year. If your thoughts do not produce fruitage, then change your seed thoughts. If you are going in the right direction and your thoughts are bringing positive results, then be encouraged and stick with it. In time a rich and rewarding harvest will be there.

Focus on the Summit, the Peak of Your Being

When we are focused, the body is charged with energy. When our eye is single, one-pointed, the whole body is full of light. Then we can consciously see what we are really doing.

How do you build a muscle? Through countless repetitions against resistance. Apply that law of countless repetition to the wandering and resisting mind, and you will build discipline. As an example, your thoughts about your environment often determine how safe you are. Uncontrolled, undisciplined wandering thoughts lead people to the slums. Weak thoughts create a weak creation. Think with clear, concise, isolated thoughts and the "faucet" turns on — and the flow of abundant life is right before you.

Fill Yourself with Thoughts of Joy

Joy is an effect, and achievement is the cause, but you cannot have a deep-seated sense of fulfillment without an increased degree of consciousness. What is your view of pleasure? There is a sense of pleasure associated with being conscious and an array of unfulfilling, dulled sensations associated with lesser states of conscious awareness. For personal growth to take place, it is good to examine the reasons certain things are pleasurable. Ask, "What is its motivation?" High achievement celebrates itself with a certain resultant joy that goes far beyond physical sensations of pleasure. Examine the reason certain things are a pleasure for you. Where is the motive? Pleasure is celebrating high achievement. There are so many avenues that have life-affirming effects.

Do not listen to negative lyrics in your head. Many of them have been programmed in and others you have chosen. The more that is going wrong in your life, the more negative the lyrics are likely to be. The more constructive your ideas, the more joyful your life will be.

Whatever it is, music, thoughts, food or words, if they are not rich in meaning, why allow yourself to be consumed by them? The mind is neutral until we put something in it, programming our circumstances. It is a very heavy load for our body to carry when we hold negative lyrics in our head. Even when you have bright and focused thoughts and can slow them down, it will still require a lot of work before you begin to see the spaces of consciousness in the background. But when you do, you will begin seeing the glimmerings of who you are and where you came from.

We have a gift called life, tools called thoughts, an energy called consciousness, and the ability to create a world of our choosing.

We Choose the Wheat or the Weeds

Our aura, that energy field of color and vibration around us, is largely determined by our thoughts. If you cannot see the colors, look at the clothes that people primarily wear over time, and you will see many of those colors in the aura. A thought has color, and your thoughts surround you. Dark spots or muddy reds in the aura indicate the parts of the body that are ailing and sick.

It is our thoughts that make an area sick and create an ailment in the body. There are no accidents when it comes to illness, there is only cause and effect. Make sure you choose the cultivated wheat thoughts or the weeds will take over in uncontrolled growth.

Your Thoughts Can Be Projected Anywhere

Think positively about people, even when they are at a distance, and the energy around them will expand when your positive thoughts hit them. Hopefully their aura will light up.

Astral projection is as simple as a projection of your thoughts. It does not have to be a part of you physically. Your consciousness can reach to the stars and travel at the speed of light. When you astral-project your focus, you are connected beyond time and space.

Dark Designs Always Boomerang

Evil can be powerful, but it can never triumph over the truth. We cannot afford to have dark designs or unhealthy thoughts. People who have discordant energy cause static pollution around them. The brain's electrical signals travel through air and space. A high energy thought pattern can travel around the world and back.

Do you have demons or angels around you? Just examine your thoughts and you'll find out. Demons are your dark thoughts, confused thoughts, scattered thoughts and irrational thoughts. Darkness starts with a malfunctioning mind. What you entertain in your mind is what you get. Do you hold angelic aspirations or demonic designs? You create heaven or hell with your thoughts. If thoughts were entities, what kind of gatherings would you have?

Demons are the darkness, and darkness is the opposite of light. Evil is a self-fulfilling prophecy fueled by lies. When the sun comes out, Mr. Darkness runs away and hides. When the dirt is taken away, the gold of your aura will shine.

Luminous Thoughts

Just like the sun is needed for growth, so are bright thoughts. Thoughts are luminous and bright when they support what you find valuable in life. You have the right to pursue happiness on earth, here and now. To accomplish this you must use your mind clearly and concisely. As you believe, so it is for you. We have a gift called life, tools called thoughts, an energy called consciousness, and the ability to create a world of our choosing.

Be luminous within yourself.

QUESTIONS AND ANSWERS

How is it that you know what we are thinking? How about that Christmas Eve? I recall sitting at home, wishing you and Ann a Merry Christmas in my heart. You called, laughing, and said, "I just told Ann, 'John's coming through, I'd better run downstairs and call him.'"

Does a mother know when her baby stirs at night?

Ah, I love you, Peter. Thank you for my tears. You often state that thought is creative, and you have encouraged us to use the affirmation, "What you want, wants you." Can you explain how that happens?

It's all very scientific. In physics there is a basic law of electromagnetic attraction that goes like this: Wherever you have an electrical field, you will also have a corresponding magnetic field which produces a very powerful electromagnetic attraction. To demonstrate, all you need do is rapidly spin magnets past one another in opposing directions, and have a copper coil to catch and direct the produced current of electricity. It is simple and mystical at the same time — much like thought energy.

We are the sum total of our thoughts, and those very thoughts have become the "shaper" of our reality, the creator of our circumstances and the very "molder" of our karma. Thoughts, like magnets, attract and draw to us not so much what we want as much as that which we truly are. Yes, what you want — deeply from within —wants you! That deep subconscious drive, that deep electromagnetic power, has been shaped and molded by trillions of conscious and unconscious thoughts. Even bad dreams build power to create bad events.

To use thought properly, it must be channeled just as a copper wire is used to direct the current to an appliance. If the current is allowed to jump and spark undirected, well... consider just a little gas leaking from the kitchen stove, or frayed wires hidden in the wall of an old house. I believe you have the picture. Thought must be purposeful and direct. No live wires should be left lying around in our head. We are not wired to allow our thoughts to be plugged into every socket of our undirected imagination, fantasies or daydreams. If we do, we will blow up the circuits of our body's energy centers.

Understand, our thought world is so powerful that we can even use it to blow ourselves up. We are only as safe as our thoughts. Yet consider, your flesh is just frozen memory waiting to be thawed, and the thoughts released wait to go forth and gather either blessings or curses.

What do you mean by "our bodies being frozen memory?"

Good body workers, from masseurs to point holding therapists, have experienced a client suddenly expressing emotionalized memories; memories they were totally unconscious of until certain acupressure points were touched. With very powerful people, their patients' emotions can often be released by a simple hug or just the touch of a hand.

The analogy can be drawn between the body's energy field and a holographic film plate. The film plate can be cut in half, and then when a laser light is focused on it, it will still project a total three-dimensional image. Cut the plate one hundred times, take the tiniest piece and focus light through it, and you will still project the original picture. In the physical body, every cubic centimeter contains the total image of the complete physical and spiritual form as well as containing the frozen thoughts needed to resurrect a perfect spiritual being, alive in pristine purity. As many times as we mar the plate with corrupt, servile and impotent images, the film retains the image of perfection; yet, with each scratch it will be duller and more removed from the original.

We have degenerated light years away from the legend of our ancestors, the immortal, sun-kissed, breatharian gods, only to find ourselves groveling as a disease-ridden race. So many are unable to hold a single thought of luminous perfection longer than a fleeting second, and yet, the ancient master would again remind us, "Have you not heard, ye are gods?"

As we clean the cobwebs from both body and mind, somehow the statement appears to hold a strange familiarity. I say, may the ancient echoes tear apart the rags of limitation and give you the courage to wake and walk forth from the cave of death into the sun of light and immortal life.

A friend asks this question: "There are times when a scenario I focus upon and plan for does not materialize, yet something else does that is usually beneficial but totally unexpected. Sometimes the unexpected is even better — which is a good thing. But I am uncertain how to visualize. Am I being too specific in my thinking or not specific enough?"

I would say, both. This is an excellent and well-worded question. First, we must examine the premise on which questions of this nature sit; then I can answer you in a more clear and understandable manner. Here's the bottom line: People who have clear-cut goals and people who do not, both suffer. Both are plagued with an undercurrent of chronic anxiety. The goal-setting individual has more stimulating and fulfilling experiences in this life. Yet, both remain unhappy. Of course, some will vehemently deny this. They don't want to expose the fact that they are fools.

Our thoughts, both focused and unfocused, produce self-fulfilling prophecies. And yes, we get what we set. I've said it many times: You can't hit a target you cannot see. So, now that you've won first place — hit the bull's-eye — what now? As soon as the excitement has worn off, you are again on the run for newer and better experiences. And remember the faster you run, the faster you must, for you are only chasing an illusion, a shadow of the reality, not the real thing.

You are correct in saying, "Sometimes the unexpected is even better." The old, the planned for, has become stale in our minds. So, the subconscious surprises us with something "totally unexpected." Like the person who constantly visualized counting out stacks of hundred dollar bills and ended up as a bank teller. Or, the man who visualized himself sailing on a large ship to the South Pacific, only to discover he was on a troop ship sailing to Vietnam. Be very specific and detailed, and yet understand what you truly require, for your growth will manifest within these conditions.

Yes, you can change the people, places and things in your life. You can be very effective and skillful in accomplishing this. Yet, no matter who you are with, or where you are, you will still be working out the laws of cause and effect, not only from today, yesterday, last year or so on, but even further back than that.

My advice is to cut the desires to a minimum. Live deliberately and simply and set only goals that uncomplicate. Set goals for greater serenity, quietude, seclusion and peace. Seek to create an environment which is more conducive to the joyous purpose for which we have been born. Seek that which does not die. Seek what thieves cannot steal, moths consume, or rust tarnish. Seek first the kingdom of consciousness and then all these other trinkets shall be yours as well. Seek deep into the depths of your own heart and its desires, and you will find there is only one.

Health

Healing Yourself

Love Heals, Rejuvenates and Mends All the Broken Parts

Healing occurs with love. It is love that is the healer and it is love that removes all that is not wanted. Peter once said, "I have the ability to love you so much that it is impossible for you to be sick in my presence." Many difficulties just simply go away when you are in a holy place. You may pull the difficulties back to you when you leave a holy space, but by loving yourself and allowing yourself to be loved, you can begin to accept the gift of having all illnesses healed.

We are healed by being loved. God is love, and love is the only God. Where you feel love, there is healing.

Hope Is a Wonderful, Creative Force That Can Heal

There is a divine presence and energy with tremendous power. All the help one could ever imagine is available. Do all you can and the divine will take care of the rest. But, you must first do all you can. You cannot get by with seeking excuses rather than working on yourself.

Hope is this trust that there is a divine healing energy, and then the hope and trust turn into knowingness. Evidence can be found all around us. Hope is faith looking forward. It heals because it is a loving and comforting thought, thus a creative force in positive emotions.

Some will place their hope in crystals, angels and saints. Some are authentic and others are projections; yet, we may all experience the divine in personal ways.

It Is the Fragrance of the Flower That Heals

It is not the flower that heals. Rather, it is the fragrance of the flower, the "God scent," that lives in your consciousness that heals. This God scent creates a charged electrical field. It is this field that keeps us healthy and whole.

Being aware of the God scent involves being conscious of being conscious. Seek it. Accept responsibility, which means you have the ability to respond to life. Can you respond to change or difficulties as challenges rather than tragedies?

When the mind is clear, the body becomes clear also. When you feel love, others will sense your electromagnetic field and feel safe around you. Cleansing the negative thoughts creates a harmonious field of attraction.

Your Mind Is More Powerful Than You May Have Imagined

What you perceive about yourself is always true because, given time, you make it true. Do not hold to dark thoughts because they are registered as a trauma in every cell of your body. Watch that you only hold positive thoughts of yourself and believe in an energy inside that always takes care of you. Believe that you will always come out safe.

Do not focus on heart attacks or cancer or liver damage or aging. Deal with the facts. The facts are that you are being made whole each second. Just don't interfere; the body knows what it is doing.

Deal With the Facts, Not the Emotions

Health operates optimally with the facts; deal with them. You can look at illness holistically or allopathically. Decide which approach will work for you. Look for the facts, then make a decision and don't worry about it.

Don't waver. Wavering is one of the worst things for health, especially cancer. Be consistent and decisive. Whether you go to allopathic or holistic practitioners, remember you cannot ride two horses at the same time. Don't be a hypocrite, you can't do both. Yes, your choices do matter. Often it's a choice between life and death. Do what is right for you. The person who chooses to live does so by examining the facts of what is right for him or her.

Be Feisty

Spontaneous remissions result from a deep-seated decision to live. Being worried is the opposite of being feisty, and it is the same as death. Life requires being a little feisty. If we just do as we're told, we lose our energy, for we don't need any when others are making decisions for us.

Live your own life. Make decisions on how to improve any given situation and your health will improve. It is inaction that does you in. Make your own decisions. Stand your ground, and you'll soon discover that feisty equals a healing personality.

Heal Yourself, Or Find Someone Who Can Help You

The human spirit can heal all things. If you cannot heal yourself, then go to the next step and find someone who can help you heal yourself. Seek a professional when you cannot fix it yourself. To the degree that our energy is high we can send healing. People heal themselves, but another highly energized person can push you into a healing.

Look for the Good in Others

Tremendous energy can be generated through the tone of our voice, and this energy can help people heal. There is a payoff in our physical health when we look for the good in someone else. You may not like a given person's personality, but there is likely to be something positive in them that you can look for and fan into something bigger. Look for the light side, not for the dark. You do not have to like or respect everyone, but as long as you are in their company, focus on their positive characteristics rather than their annoying ones.

There Are Two Types of People — Positive and Negative

What we truly are determines how we respond to the world. Our circumstances in life show the world what we have been thinking and what our expectations are. Our circumstances are a result of what we have thought. The positive person will be able to direct her body to heal because she has a vested interest in being healed. If you don't see yourself as whole, you'll be sick.

If You're Not Getting Better, You May Be Getting Bitter

Believing we are always improving allows us to create more harmony. If we are bitter, we will not get better. Solve the problems of the world by not being a problem yourself. This is in your own best interest if you want a positive healthy reality.

The Aura Is Our Spiritual Skin

Our thoughts create colors which are spun off and seen in our auras. The aura is the spiritual "skin" that projects what is inside. It is like the atmosphere around the earth, it protects us from interference just as the atmosphere protects the earth from radiation. The higher our thoughts, the more refined our aura will be. The higher our energy, the more protected we are from the turbulence of the world.

When our mental body experiences emotional storms, we can easily predict physical illness and even identify the area of our body that will be affected. The aura around that body area will develop cloudiness and a change in temperature.

This can be photographed by a special technique called Kirlian photography.

The electrical force field of the aura around us can be measured. It is similar to the electrical field that can be created by friction in a balloon that will cling to a child's shirt. The same electrical field is around the body, and at times the static in it will make things cling to us that we do not want. Even the thoughts and ideas of others can literally stick to us, so guard your associations. Static electricity is made up of positive ions, and when in abundance, they trigger illness.

Healers will find clouds in the aura and take this putty-like stickiness out of the electrical field with the magnetic energy of their hands. When the aura is murky we can imagine and physically draw the hands over the body, without touching, to get the stickiness pulled off. After you pull it off with your hands, go rinse them in cold running water. This healing process is like a cosmic AAA charging our battery. Each of the human cells is like a battery with a negative and positive charge.

Jesus was so full of healing energy that it radiated from his body and many people were healed. Your body can heal others with the positive energy of life and love.

If you are doing a lot of touch therapy, wash up to the elbow and then shake the water droplets from your hands before drying them. The shaking motion helps get rid of the negative energy you may have picked up. Teach people how to heal themselves so that they are not dependent on you for a recharge. The miracle is allowing others to find ways of charging themselves.

We Live In a Bell Jar

An experiment was done regarding a toxic environment and birds. A bird was put into a bell glass with three hours' worth of oxygen. In two hours the bird was removed and another bird put in. The second bird died instantly because of the toxins. With the first bird, the toxins built up gradually over time and its body adapted. The second bird's system was shocked by the immediacy of the toxic environment.

We live in a bell jar. There is a law of vital adaptation. Many things occur gradually over the years, and our body adapts because it wants to live. We must reverse this toxic state so we don't just adapt to a toxic environment. We must change our physical and mental environment to one more pure. In order to live in a poisonous environment, we make an adaptation, but each time we do, we take another step downward. We must exert ourselves and step up to the luminous life.

Cleanse Yourself Mentally and Physically

You cannot have a clean body without a clear mind. Cleansing crises are sometimes necessary. Tissues in the body release toxins into the bloodstream and then give them off through the pores. Cleansing crises are like getting sick in reverse. You take care of the toxins before the toxins do you in. Make cleansing your body a worship of health.

Always start cleansing processes gradually. There are many helpful tinctures that assist in throwing off toxins. First, begin by juice fasting for three to four then perhaps seven to ten days. After following this type of fast, one might want to advance to a more powerful method, nature's best fast, which is a pure-water fast for the same periods of time. When doing a water fast, never use tap water. Remember, caution is in order. If you've never done a three-day fast, don't start with a seven-to-ten day fast. And if you've never done a juice fast, don't start with a water fast.

Drink chlorophyll daily. Chlorophyll transmutes its chemical structure in the bloodstream. Chlorophyll has magnesium as its central atom whereas the hemoglobin in our blood has iron as its central atom, but once chlorophyll enters the body it becomes blood by an amazing process of transmutation. Chlorophyll is important for the blood because it detoxifies it. It also changes the pH balance of saliva and is great for the teeth because the saliva becomes more alkaline, thus preventing decay and gum problems.

All green plants have chlorophyll, that's what makes them green. Eat lots of sprouts and green, raw matter in salads. Sprouts are highly magnetic and provide tremendous energy that charges the body. Blue-green algae are great for the system as well as many other chlorophyll-rich algae.

How To Get Rid of Bad Habits

Good habits set you free. Bad habits enslave. The way you play the game of life is through nonaddiction. Change old, negative habits. Use the law of substitution, which is to replace every negative thought and inclination with a deliberate positive thought and positive motivation. This requires exercise and practice. Every given moment you have a choice. You are not without power. Get into the driver's seat. It is do-able. Substitute the new for the old.

Focus on the Beautiful

As you think, a certain sensation from those thoughts actually massages your heart. This is what is meant by the singing of the heartstrings. When the mind is healthy, the heart is healthy.

Focus on the beautiful but know also that the world is full of contrast. And be not dismayed when you seek diamonds hidden among the stones. Life is a yin and yang balancing act that is delicate. It is said that it is so delicate that a feather can move a thousand pounds. Why would we allow ourselves to feast our eyes upon that which is not healing? We have choices as to what we look at and these choices heal or destroy us. Develop a powerful love of life. Chances are you won't die if you still have a love of life and have things to do. Don't postpone being happy. Feast your eyes upon that which is healing.

Even in the harsh and ugly, seek the beautiful that may be hidden in it.

We Are Responsible for our Body's Health

You complicate your life if you don't feel worthy of being healthy and happy. We are responsible for our body's health. When we believe in living with high ideals, we add "oomph" to our "try" and we have "triumph" over our challenges. Look into your own two eyes and say, "I am responsible. What am I going to do about it? If it's to be, it's up to me." Do not ask for anyone to live for you, and don't feel obligated to live for anyone else. You really can only live your own life. As you guide your mind into self-responsible thought patterns, you will create an unparalleled life.

Focus on being worthy of health. Know that healing of health issues does not occur overnight. Various high states of health may take years to obtain, but remember, the time is going to pass anyway, so why not commit the time to creating health?

The Gestures of Happiness Can Bring Healing

When we are stressed frequently or intensely, our adrenal glands are taxed and may begin to malfunction. Institutionalized people with particular thinking patterns have a certain look because their glands have been malfunctioning, causing profound changes in the physical gestures and mannerisms.

People, like plants, start to droop when they don't feel good. Their hair loses its luster and becomes dull. Sickness and expiration come from too much seriousness and not enough sincerity. When you become lighthearted, you are filled with light and it is difficult to be with friends or family who make everything a serious issue. As you brighten up you'll find yourself laughing more.

Health: Healing Yourself

If you know you need to relax, do so, and all things will heal. If you are overworked, stop it. If you are underworked, go to work. You only get tired when you do what you don't want to do.

Also, learn this sacred secret: Change what is taxing you if you are overstressed. Enough is enough. Rest and revamp your attitudes. Smile more. Discover something funny about life and you will start improving your health and well-being. Laughter gives inspiration. As an experiment, attempt to laugh for 15 minutes straight. This will stimulate the thymus gland and increase your vitality.

Creative Visualization

What you see is what you get. When you visualize yourself in a positive light, all the negative symptoms go away. When you see clearly mentally, you will feel your body energy flowing through all the meridians. When confused, residue crystals can develop, crystallizing the meridians or the nerve pathways and blocking the energy flow in your body. There are acupressure points that can be held to dissolve these crystals. For example, from the viewpoint of acupressure, the big toe represents the head. You can stimulate areas of the head by holding points on the toe such as the ones to stimulate the pituitary, pineal and hypothalamus gland.

The fingers also have various pressure points, and we can apply firm pressure on those areas and discover crystals that need to be dissolved. As pressure is applied to the crystallized point, it will become intensely hot and melt like ice beneath the finger. Every part of one's body has pressure points that indicate the health of the individual.

Our bodies will glow like a wonderful light and health will be obvious to all when freed from encumbrances and blockages.

Energy Vampires

Some people are energy vampires. They cling and are parasitic and you feel drained when you are around them. Say no to interactions with them. You will feel good when around others with positive energy. Recharging oneself calls for sufficient alone time, being still. There is no limit to the energy in the universe, but there is a switch — a regulator to that flow of unlimited energy. Stillness is the key.

If you have physical contact with lots of people, and they have negative energy or even negative talk, immediately wash your hands and shake them off. Wash your face with cool running water, too. Cold water is more invigorating and charges you more. Do your best to keep your distance from negative people in the first place.

Right after a serious, life-negating conversation, go take a cold shower. At the very least, wash your hands with cold water. We collect static in our energy field (aura) and running water will help clear it. When feeling sick or out of sorts, start smiling. This stimulates the thymus gland which in turn stimulates the immune system. There are nerve endings that connect the muscles of the face to the immune system. Often we find that serious people cannot laugh. Lighthearted people laugh easily. Don't take life so seriously. Smile and laugh, and your immune system will be strengthened. There is nothing as healing as a hearty laugh.

The Universe of Energy

Think of yourself as a fish swimming in a universe of energy. The air around us is like a net made of electrical fibers and woven magnetism. As we allow ourselves to flow more and to give up biased judgment and fears, we develop mentally and emotionally and become healthier. Our faces start to change and our organs change too. When we are in balance with the energy of the universe, we fill out or thin down physically to reach our body's balance.

> *God is love, and love is the only God.*
> *Where there is love, there is healing.*

QUESTIONS AND ANSWERS

Peter, several friends have asked the cause of cancer, particularly breast cancer. Would you share your thoughts on this?

I can certainly appreciate their concern. There appears to be a breast cancer epidemic as it is the leading cause of death in women between the ages of thirty-five and fifty-five. I have read that more women have died of breast cancer than all the Americans killed in combat in all of our recent wars combined, from WWI to Desert Storm. Even so, those horrendous statistics should not scare us. Nature always has a remedy. There are no problems without solutions. I firmly believe that all disease is mental first. Change your mind and you'll change matter.

Since many want a supplement, a magic bullet, some type of pill instead of working on the mental body, I'll make it very simple — consume garlic! Volumes have been written about the inhibitory influence of garlic on both breast and prostate cancer cells. Eat plenty of fresh, raw, smelly, hot garlic cloves and drink copious amounts of fresh, raw, organic carrot, broccoli and cabbage juice and you'll not have a thing to worry about except your head.

I have read a study where EPA, eicosapentaenoic acid indole-3-carbinol, resulted in an up to 99 percent inhibition of cancer cells of both breast and prostate. EPA is what's in cabbage and broccoli juice. Now let's look at the cause of cancer.

Cancer or any other disease always has the same basic cause. For simplicity's sake, let us consider that a person has three bodies, though there are actually more. The first is a mental body, second an energy body, and third a physical body. Now, I don't think that anyone would disagree that our thoughts affect our energy, and our energy affects our physical state. Have you ever been in a situation where you experienced great fear? Perhaps it was the first time you looked down from a great height and felt your legs get rubbery as your heart pounded loudly in your chest. What did the fear do to your energy? Or how has your physical body felt after a bout of intense anger? What about the emotions you experience when you feel trapped in an unpleasant relationship, oppressive job or an unhealthy environment? Isn't it as if some invisible octopus with its far-reaching tentacles has its suction cups draining out every bit of your energy? When you feel this state of helplessness, frustration and anger, you are being stalked by cancer.

There is nothing new about cancer. Cancer is as old as astrology where it gets its name,

Cancer the crab. It was known to Hippocrates, Galen and many other ancient physicians. They saw this disease spread like a crab with legs going in all directions. I find it very much like the Cancer personality with its scattered concerns going in opposite directions at the same time. Anger and frustration, coupled with haste and anxiety, equal consuming stress that results in cancer.

Just like concerns that are divorced from controls, the consuming stress seeks to find a release valve, and when it cannot find one, it initiates a self-destructive process. When the mental body is confused by conflicting and contradictory thoughts and conclusions, it passes the skewed messages to the brain and the control center of the pituitary gland which in turn signals the immune system via the thymus gland. The irrationality of the message stops the immune system in its tracks. Often when the thymus gland does send out its warriors, the T cells, B cells, macrophages and lymphocytes, they are confused as to which cells are friends or foes and attack healthy cells. The crab grows larger and becomes even more powerful.

Like everything in the world of nature, including the cells of our bodies, growth is essential to survival. However, excessive growth beyond the balanced state of maturity results in imbalances and abnormal growth. Such growth in abnormal directions results in tumors. When the growth is unorganized they are neoplasms. When nature's balance has been violated, these cells propagate at criminal levels, invading areas of the body that are unable to repel these attackers. These law-breakers are malignant tumors. When these anarchistic cells have entered or invaded other body sites, they have metastasized.

Once we have lost our balanced state of being and are mentally bounced around helter-skelter in all directions, the ground is ripe for cancer. When our obsession for wealth, name, fame or power consumes us, we are then ripe for cancer also.

I once had a friend who was a very wealthy businessman. He was attempting to go through a divorce, build a new factory and oversee a large subdivision development at the same time. He soon discovered that his body was consumed with cancer. He was not aware of how his lifestyle affected his health. His particular lifestyle was one that resembled a crab with legs going in all directions, so much so that he was unable to go forward and was bound to move sideways.

This friend called me one morning. I asked him about his day and he told me this was his fortieth phone call that morning. I asked, "Where are you?" He answered, "Sitting on the commode in the bathroom." I told him that out of caring and concern for him I was hanging up. I knew this man was not going to live if he continued being consumed by pressure. When he was told he had only a few months at most to live, he asked me what I thought about him taking his yacht and cruising down the Mississippi River to New Orleans, something he had always wanted to do. I told him it would give him a break from his consuming affairs and an opportunity to heal himself. My friend seemed pleased but regretted, he "couldn't afford the time." He never took the trip and died in the hospital wired up to feeding tubes and other devices. I thought, could it be that these words will be engraved on his headstone: "He couldn't afford the time?"

There is a psychological profile to every cancer. Breast cancer entails a long history of not feeling nourished or loved. Therefore, the woman feels unable to give nourishment and/or have her love accepted by others. Mothers, daughters and granddaughters form a long string of dysfunctional relationships of this nature. The heredity of this cancer is as much a mental construct as it is a biological event.

Poverty is also a contributing factor which results from a "not enough milk" perception. Breast cancer is not a breast-size issue. Even large breasts can be stingy, a result of poverty consciousness. Cultural beliefs about a woman's attractiveness were often based on her breasts in hunter/gatherer societies, so much so that well-endowed women were often considered better providers of milk for the offspring. This same misconception continued to prevail in modern society, thus a breast fixation. Women who believed they were unattractive to the opposite sex and harbored lifelong anxiety over the issue, increased their likelihood of creating breast cancer. How many years of disliking the size and shape of their breasts did it take to develop a cancer that would result in the chopping off and devastating destruction of that very breast? What you don't like becomes vulnerable to the unconscious creation of disease in that area.

In a man, prostate cancer may be due in part to not feeling that he is fulfilling his role as a provider. He may not have the "balls" to stand up to what he believes in or the ability to do so. The man may feel any criticism about his sexual performance too deeply. These are largely subconscious issues. Not being able to reconcile or hold onto the issues deep in the subconscious ocean may result in a man's inability to hold his water, that is, to control his bladder, a major warning sign of prostate problems.

First, the solution for the mental body is to work on establishing a positive self-image and cultivating strong self-esteem. Second, you do not have to live your life by another's script for you. You are not here to be a servant. You are here to become a master, lord of your personal world. You are here to free yourself from the trivial things the mob races to attain. You are here to live your own life, a life lived deliberate-

ly by your choosing. You are here to have your circle of concern and your circle of control match. What is in your sphere of influence? Drop worrying about what is not in this sphere of influence. You are here to say what you please without remorse or anger consuming you. You are here to climb your own mountain and not to stumble over the hills of others. You are here to find meaning, fulfillment and purpose in your life. And, most of all, you are here to live!

Embrace the luminous, purposeful life, the liberated life, and never again will you grovel before disease.

Peter, what can you do to prevent cancer from becoming fatal when it is diagnosed?

Avoid the diagnosis. I find it incredible that we accept a diagnosis from a person who in many cases barely knows us and our bodies. How is it that we know so little of the messages our bodies have been giving us; and yet, in a few minutes and after a few tests, "the experts" come up with a diagnosis?

Dia is a Greek prefix that means "through

or across" and gnosis *means "to recognize." It comes from the Greek* gnosis *or Latin* gnosco *or* nosco, *"to inquire into." It was also the ancient capital of Crete. We also get the Greek word* agnostic *or "unknowing" from the same root word* agnostos. *So often, in their "unknowing," they proclaim the sentence of death as swiftly as an ancient deity would proclaim punishment for a lawbreaker. How often their savage cries are self-fulfilling prophecies — that being the only power of the diagnosis.*

Just the other day a close friend of ours was in a terrible accident in which her husband was killed and she barely survived. A doctor at the hospital noticed that her ankle was infected and told her that it would be best to amputate her foot. She called me and related the doctor's diagnosis. The doctor had told her that the infection might spread and the amputation was necessary. I replied, "In my mind, chopping off a foot isn't an option. If I had an infected fingernail, what would be easier to do — clear up the infection or grow a new finger?" I thought, "This doctor is utterly insane, and if not insane, then this person must have been asking which option would result in more monetary gain — amputation or an antibiotic." If this second were the case, the doctor needs to be thrown in prison, and if not, then the nut house.

A friend arranged for another doctor to care for her and flew her to a second hospital with confidence that she would keep her foot, and she did.

So, choose your poison. How about the options of slash, cut or burn? I assure you, if you cut off your head you'll never have headaches again. Pull all your teeth and I promise you'll never have another toothache. Cut off your toe and you'll never have another hangnail. Cut off your breast and you'll never have another tumor, benign or malignant. So, choose your poison or choose your cure.

The good news is, if you have caused your disease, you can cure it. The bad news is, if you didn't cause your disease, you can't do a thing about it. If you hold the second belief, you can then helplessly assert, "I am a victim."

I am convinced that there are no victims, only volunteers. If I am correct, then you are the physician and nature is the pharmacopoeia. In the living book of nature is found everything and anything; but before you can avail yourself of her amazing array of cures, you must, I repeat, you must get your head in the right space.

Just as you can't ride two horses at the same time, you cannot take the conventional medical route and nature's way at the same time. You must be 100 percent committed to one path or the other before you even begin. If you choose nature's way, just like the biblical story of Lot's wife, you must not ever at any time ever look back. You have made your choice in the face of death, and now resolutely and courageously you must go forward without hesitation. I will tell you today, you will look death in the eye and fearlessly go on.

You must also realize you may not be successful. You may even lose your battle. But, even so, you must not turn around. If you do, then any slim chance of winning will be lost. This is very difficult for many because they have never been totally committed to anything in their lives to this point. Today you must begin anew. You must vow to yourself as in songwriter Hal

Wilson's lyrics, "I'd rather drown than turn around." You must then journey one step after the other, one day at a time. Your goal must be to have more good days than bad days even though setbacks will assault you along this perilous path. But in full trust and confidence you will remind yourself, "by the inch it's a cinch, by the yard it's hard."

If a complete, unwavering and focused commitment to healing is made, you will survive. If your commitment is only 90 percent, then you have only a 90 percent chance. If your commitment is only 50 percent, then your survival is a coin toss, and if you choose slash and burn... then get your affairs in order today.

Most likely, if you have been led to consider my words, then you are a different spirit. My words are like fire and have the power to melt your chains. When you are ablaze with this healing flame, no person, no place, no thing can stop you. You are the power, you are the light and you are the cure. The divine is the promise that does not fail!

* * *

As to nature's way, utilize a 90 percent fresh and raw diet of organic fruits and vegetables. Drink plenty of fresh juiced carrots, beets and other vegetables. Please note, you cannot heal without a juicer, period! Buy one now if you don't have one.

Consume garlic and cayenne peppers by the truckload. Utilize slippery elm and aloe for poultices as these poultices assist the regrowth of healthy tissue. Comfrey, echinacea, red clover, goldenseal, lobelia and many other fresh herbs are powerful in destroying cancer. Remember, you are responsible for doing the homework and educating yourself. There are many excellent books on natural healing. Read them, digest them and apply them and you will without a doubt heal. You must never expect another to do for you what you are unwilling to do for yourself. Be creative and rational in how you find your resources. So plan your work and work your plan. Get busy now!

Peter, would it be possible to include a comment on infants and children with cancer?

It is difficult to say how many hearts ache when confronted with caring for a little one in that condition. Every day one is faced with uncertainty and anxiety over the fate of the child. The child, on the other hand, is in some manner attempting to answer the question of why this has happened. Here we have a classic example of the two questions that appear to haunt the majority of earth's inhabitants, "What if?" and "Why?"

I have found that the dawn of wisdom arrives when those two questions dissolve in the recognition of "Now" and "It is." Someone phrased it cleverly in "Today is the tomorrow you hoped for yesterday." Or the tomorrow that was feared, the tomorrow that was dreaded, but none the less, is manifest here and now.

When futuring and pasting are dropped and this moment is totally embraced with full consciousness and intensity, we are free to entertain the joys and blessings that dance before our eyes each second anew. Each spring as I await the birth of flower blossoms in my garden, I am not depressed by the thought of their transitory existence. The fact that they will only be with me for a season and pass only intensifies their beauty. The beautiful butterfly sitting on my head this moment will fly away and one day never return. One must not miss each second's opportunity to celebrate the beautiful, the pure and the innocent.

I cannot begin to tell you of the many pets, both domestic and wild, I have lost and how many tears have moistened my cheeks as they, like the flowers, pass through their seasons. And yet, tears of joy fill me with the intense richness they have added to my life. I have allowed both their entrance and exit and allowed the river of life to freely flow through my heart on to the ocean of eternity. In that river are reflected millions of faces like my own. They ebb and flow, blur and blend, all in some strange way alike and yet different. Faces of friends long lost, children I played ball with and pushed on swings, the folks whose arms held me and rocked me to sleep as a child, people I fought and argued with, people I loved and people I had hated —

all of them blended into one flow of life, one experience of being.

And you ask for me to comment on children with cancer? How can I do so without including all? For they, like the butterflies fluttering around on tender flower blossoms in their momentary dance, are our teachers. When our minds shout, "Unfair!" our hearts melt with compassion, and when the heart cries, we wash ourselves inside out. The dust of judgment and demand and the desire that it be otherwise are washed away in the river of acceptance, the river of life eternal. Only in this flow are we free.

It is as it is and we are where we are — find that spot and you will have gone to heaven.

NOTE: This chapter relates the thoughts and actions of Peter concerning healing. It is not recommended that the information be used without consulting a medical professional.

What Causes Illness and Accidents?

You Create Diseases — You Don't Catch Them

All of the comforts of life do no good if you are too sick to enjoy them. Pain is sickness and sickness is pain. All illness is no more than the energy we expend to hold onto negative thoughts. Don't focus on illness, focus on health. The electricity of your thoughts will heal you or kill you. What you are thinking can change the state of your health so quickly. If you vividly imagine something, you holographically create it. How we see ourselves is how we become.

If your consciousness diminishes, your health diminishes. When conscious we can remember, perceive, reason and not be confused. You will not succumb to disease if anxiety, apprehension, depression and fear are absent. A state of illness will appear when we hold "stinking thinking" through "pasting and futuring." Depression comes with living in the dead past and anxiety results from anticipating an unsure future. Stay in the present moment, for only that is real.

Everything in the universe works in harmony with the law of cause and effect, and if a positive cause is violated you get sickness, the negative effect. If you are sick, you are choosing the effect consciously or unconsciously. Figure out the pattern, and you discover the cause. Everything in the universe works in harmony with cause and effect, so you choose your sickness or your health.

Your ability to think clearly and differentiate between that which is true and that which is false is a necessity for health.

Memory, Belief and Health

All disease is mental first. The immune system is your memory and your memory is your immune system. As memory fails, so does your immune system. It forgets what it's supposed to do; it sometimes forgets what is friendly and what is not. It sometimes cannot identify what is pro-life or anti-life in attitudes and beliefs. The very cells that are there to protect the body can become confused and attack other healthy cells. When our thoughts are positive, clear, concentrated and focused, there is no cellular confusion. Rational thought produces an organized immune system that never gets confused or forgets.

Memory is the result of visualization, association and the clear focusing on one thing at a time. Higher levels of the neurotransmitter, dopamine, assist in memory. Forgetfulness increases with high levels of serotonin. AIDS dementia often comes about with increased serotonin levels which appear to confuse the thymus gland and may also aggravate the expression of symptoms in Parkinson's and Alzheimer's disease.

There Are No Accidents

How do you drive a car? The saying goes, "Show me how a person drives and I'll tell you about their life." How you drive is how you live. If you go beyond your speed limit, life will create an opportunity for you to slow down. And, know that you never have an accident without being warned many little times beforehand. You can never have an accident without creating it. It is either an ordered world or an accidental world. In reality, it's a world that is ordered and operates within cause and effect. We try to rationalize accidents by claiming unawareness, but the result is actually a boomerang of our thoughts. Our thoughts inevitably come back. The higher and clearer our level of consciousness, the quicker we receive the effects of our thoughts.

Physical accidents operate under the laws of cause and effect. We even bring with us from past lives certain inclinations, traits and habits. When fears predominate, we are drawn to accidents. Our hopes and fears draw us to health or illness.

**Emotionally Turbulent Days
Create Storms in Our Auras**

Worry and emotional shock may be analogized to tossing a rock in a pond. Far after the rock sinks and the splash is gone, ripples continue. When we have emotional reactions, the ripples continue for days in the aura. Tremors go on after the emotional event is finished, and your whole body trembles like a large lump of Jell-O being carried on a plate. If you have shock after shock after shock, then the glue of your cells starts disintegrating. When trauma after trauma occurs, the mortar of your makeup begins to crumble.

Think of yourself as an electrical system. The cells of your body have a positive and a negative charge running as a current. Shocks twist them around and out of alignment; the misdirected electricity then shows up as "clouds" filled with lightning in given areas of the aura where your body is weak.

The aura is the skin of the soul and it will flare up in deep red blotches when we get irritated. A few days later, it may begin to appear on our physical skin, not just our spiritual skin. It may even begin to ulcerate the physical skin. This is when things "get under your skin." When the body is full of tension and confusion, we smother ourselves with the useless and unessential. This is how we get sick and die. Don't let things get under your skin. It's the little things that get under your skin and irritate you. Once it's seen in the auric field, it will soon be seen in your flesh. The electricity of your thoughts can heal you or kill you. As we evolve into the luminous life, petty people and petty issues do not throw us off balance.

Disease Occurs When We Are in Clouds of Negativity

Sometimes people have addictions to diseases, and if the disease is not present, they may get lonely for the familiarity of having that disease.

When we internalize, we accept responsibility for the cure, when we externalize, a doctor becomes responsible for our cure. Really, a person cures herself because she is getting the desired attention. It is this attention that cures because she feels that someone cares.

It is essential to care for ourselves. Don't make someone else responsible for your well-being. You are the healer. It is all inside. "I Am All Light. I Am My Healing."

When our auras are strong, we cannot get sick.

Sickness Will Always Follow Disoriented Thinking

Confused thinking always comes before sickness. Disoriented, irrational, confused, and illogical thoughts can cause sickness because the aura — the bio-magnetic electrical field surrounding the body — is short-circuited by cloudy thoughts of indecision and negativity. Disoriented thoughts are what cloud the light and make auras dingy and dark. When we quit watching our words and become unfocused and undirected, then our words become destructive.

The Common Cold

How much food can we put into our bodies before it has to come out? When our diet includes an abundance of mucous-forming foods like eggs, dairy products, meat and fat, we are ripe for colds. Toxins are in the mucous that is discharged. Mucus can also clog and crystallize in the body. We must cleanse ourselves to live healthy lives. At times it takes a healing crisis, which is getting sick in reverse, to rid our bodies of poisons. If what we take in clogs the colon, it clouds the eyes and mind as well. The common cold is generally no more than the body expelling mucus. At the onset of cold weather, people are said to be susceptible to colds. Actually, the cold temperature only causes the body's tissues to contract. This literally squeezes the mucus out of its many orifices.

Pain and Tendinitis

If we continue to hold on to mistaken conclusions in the face of overwhelming evidence to the contrary, we may end up with elbow, wrist, or finger pain. Tendinitis often occurs when one feels that he is forced to hold on to distressing situations, ideas, people or environments. Relax and be with the moment.

Gamma Linolenic Acid (GLA) helps when arthritis is present. GLA is found in the oil of the herb Borage, Evening Primrose and Black Current seeds. In some double-blind studies, reduction of chronic joint inflammation ran close to 50 percent by using many of these natural methods.

One of the safest and most natural ways to deal with, and minimize, physical pain is simply by raising the brain's endorphin levels. A primary way of getting the endorphins flowing is to be inspired.

Cancer

Cancer occurs when healthy cells go crazy. Cancer may start to develop when we are confused about outcomes in love and life. When we are indecisive about what to do, cell growth is disrupted. Cells lump up and form a tumor when we lack clarity about life. When one is indecisive about what to do for long periods of time, the likelihood of cell disruption may increase. Cancer is caused by free radicals and by confused, non-directed or disorganized thoughts. There has to be direction for a cell to function properly. Stop the undisciplined thinking. Start focusing on the essentials.

We Create Cancer

Don't beat yourself up if you have created cancer. The good news is: If we created it, we can cure it. If it's just something that happens, then we're doomed. The statement that "we create cancer" helps us understand that the entire human race behaves suicidally. Whenever we die, we have chosen suicide in whatever form it takes. When we are confused, a cell rebels and grows on its own, undirected. Cancer is really healthy cells in the body containing a confused mind. A cancer cell is a rebellious cell that has become confused as to how to function, much like the person who possesses the cell has become confused.

Cells that are confused about what to do become unhealthy. A one-pointed mind has a healthy body. A healthy body reflects the healthy mind. Cancer is the result of a confused, indecisive, and often angry or resentful mind set. The person who has cancer often has a personality that appears compliant — the nice guy on the outside who is raging on the inside. That conflict is what creates cancer.

The healthier approach is to say what you mean and mean what you say. Realize we are all free to express ourselves, and every one of us has the unreserved right to say no to what we don't like. When a person moves from a state of anger to apathy, that is when cancer has exerted its full grip. We must be able to get angry over our diseases, otherwise we're in apathy and will die. Anger over our disease is an indicator that the body's interferon level is exhilarated, and interferon keeps our immune system bolstered. Frequently a person makes a last-ditch effort and gets better just before death. What is happening is that this effort increases interferon which allows him to rally, but it can't be sustained.

In-depth understanding of the laws of life results in health. Without understanding the cause, we may not hit upon the solution. The cause lies always in our thoughts, which create our choices, which create our actions, which result in either health or illness.

If we created it, we can cure it.

Parkinson's Disease

Since Parkinson's disease is often diagnosed in those who have already lost approximately 80 percent of a certain type of their brain cells, it is imperative that we establish a healthy life style when we are young. You have heard it said, "Use it or lose it." This applies both physically and mentally. When you express uncontrolled muscle spasms and an unsteady gait, depression and so on, it is probably too late to begin. But even at this late stage some relief can be found through natural therapies and working to establish rational thought patterns as well as practicing memory-enhancement exercises. Begin now, for every ten years after forty it is estimated that we lose 10 percent of our neurodopamine cells.

Parkinson's disease can be eased by taking DHEA, Coenzme Q-10, Vitamin E, melatonin and acetyl-L-carnitine supplements.

Some People Think That the Only Way to Get to Heaven Is to Die, So They Get Sick

Some people teach that you will be happy after death. This is escapism. If you can't be happy now, you'll probably take those habit patterns with you. Thinking you can only be happy after death is part of an inaccurate and destructive belief system. If you lose someone close that you love, you may say you have had enough and that you want out of here, too. Subconsciously, we find ways out.

Subconsciously, we find ways to slowly kill ourselves. You might say that everyone who dies commits suicide. You make a commitment to live until you see the benefit of dying. Some people don't want to have to deal with what is here right now. Not dealing with things is always the same. Living takes skills, tools and energy as well as the ability to deal with what is going on in the present. Many choose to die rather than use those tools and apply the energy required.

Dying for some people seems to be the only way of getting relief. If one mentally dwells on dying or evil scenarios, one gets pain and sickness and suicidal thoughts may enter. If someone feels there is nothing fulfilling in his life, he will find a way to die. The times of personal darkness test your courage. They test your heart. They test your self-reliance. Courage is required for the spiritual life.

Without Inspiration, You Have Expiration

Either you will be inspired or you'll expire. You are, in fact, limitless if you will but crack the door. Inspiration charges us and makes us incredibly alive. Fear and worry change the body quickly with adrenaline dumps that eventually lead to expiration.

Accept reality as it is for the moment, for only now can you begin to change it. This will keep your heart from tearing apart in grief and despair. Embrace the present moment and you will be unbelievably empowered.

Never Give Attention to Illness

Do what you need to do for an illness and then don't give it any more attention. Pain is only a physical sensation, suffering is always mental. If you have something wrong with you, physically or mentally, change the mental picture, and you'll begin to change the physical. You have to be interested in living or your body will find a way to get you out of it. It will create a way to die.

Visualize What You Want

If you buy into terminal illness, you will own it, or better said, it will own you. If you embrace death, it will surely embrace you. The physical body's energy field is always the first indicator available. You get ill when there is static electricity in the aura. When this occurs there is usually organ degeneration. When cells are strong, there is a healthy electrical system pulsing in your aura and you cannot get sick. Visualize tumors melting away and the blood count will change.

*Remember, you are the healer.
It is all inside.*

QUESTIONS AND ANSWERS

Peter, you say there are no accidents at any level, but what about luck? What is luck? Does it really exist?

I'm glad you asked those questions. To understand the answer, we'll crack open the door to a glimpse of the Divine.

David Bohm was one of the world's greatest quantum physicists. One of the issues he wrestled with was the phenomenon of what appeared to be chaos, that is, phenomena that appeared to be unrelated to cause and effect. After much research, he concluded that there is no such thing as disorder, or "luck," only orders of infinitely higher degrees.

There is now equipment and computer software that can measure and convert chaotic phenomena (or luck) into shapes on a computer screen using mathematical analysis. Hidden patterns in what was thought to be chaos were discovered. There is a predictable regularity in chaos that can be visibly observed on the screen. Find out who, or more accurately what, is responsible for the design and you will crack open the door to the Divine.

Luck is chaos, and chaos has a pattern. Anything which has a predictable pattern and design is not chaos by the definition of the word. If there can be no causeless event in the universe, then luck does not exist. If "luck" exists, the universe does not.

When I say there are no accidents on any level, I mean there are no effects without causes, no reaping without sowing. Nothing exists independently or divorced from the whole. How can luck, its opposite, even be implied? When I say these things, people are often irritated, some even "burn." Why? Because the believer in luck does not want to feel any sense of responsibility in the unfolding of an event — especially if the luck is bad! From this juncture it is so easy to tumble into the world of denial. It's a place of drowning. No Lady Luck is coming to the rescue.

Embracing luck as a concept is a denial of our infinite divinity and power. How is this power discovered? Let me phrase it this way: The harder I work, the luckier I get. Or, "Luck is just preparation meeting opportunity."

Once, many years ago, I was a guest of some Washington, D.C., politicians. We went to a nearby horseracing track. Up in the clubhouse they wanted me to bet on the races. I refused. They said, "OK which horse do you think will win?" I picked all the winners — every race. Was I lucky? No! Intuitive? Yes! Did I have anything to lose? No. And that's part of the secret. You might inject, "nothing to lose, means not winning." When the evening ended, they insisted I accept a stack of bills so large it couldn't fit into a horse's mouth.

How can we learn from our past lives so we can constructively change patterns in this one? And, while I'm asking, are there such things as parallel lives? If so, share how we can be evolving on a number of reality planes at once?

Someone put it very colorfully, "Today is the tomorrow you hoped for yesterday." Your nowness, your today, is the only place you can learn anything. If there was something to learn from yesterday, why wasn't it done then? For yesterday was "now" just a few moments ago. If nowness is vivid and intense, so is our universal education in our present moments.

Heraclitus, the Greek sage, said, "You can't step into the same river twice." Yet this is what just about everyone attempts to do. The water is never the same water you experienced before. How can anyone learn from yesterday when they go on missing today? As an experiment I asked several people about a friend that we see almost daily. "Does he still have a beard?" They were dumbfounded to realize they weren't certain. And yet, people are so certain they were this person or that in a past life — nonsense! And then we seek out some expert. According to the Bible, Jesus put it aptly, "When the blind lead the blind, both fall into the pit." Please don't misunderstand me. I am not discounting or negating past lives or their effects on present patterns of behavior. The point is who are you to trust for accurate advice? If I tell you all Martian flying saucers are candy-striped, how can you believe or disbelieve? This is just an arbitrary claim. Only a fool would enter into a discussion over saucers being candy-striped or not. An arbitrary claim by its very nature requires no reply. So, do the ETs have beards or not? And our physical eyes have seen our friend just the other day, and people can't remember if the beard was or wasn't. And yet they are certain of what took place 2,000 years ago? Who in their right mind could conceive of having extra sensory perception when they haven't even experienced ordinary sensory perception?

It is my opinion that all this talk about past lives is just an excuse for not taking full responsibility for this one. "Oh! I have chronic backaches because I was once thrown off the great pyramid of Egypt." So fix it and stop your whining about the dead past — real or imag-

ined. We are so predictable. We are repeaters, habitual and so easy to read. Just note your behavior patterns and activity for the day in reverse at the close of the day and you'll discover a pattern of a lifetime. If the effects are not to your liking, simply change the causes. Thought is the cause. Experience is the effect. Awareness is the solution.

As to parallel lives, Buddha was once asked a similar question. "If a man is shot with a poisoned arrow, what should he do?" Buddha responded, "Take the poisoned arrow out before you consider anything else." Aren't we schizophrenic enough? Why not stop suffering in this life first? Just take the poisoned arrow out!

Food and Health

Eating Energy

The nutritional value of food is really in its electromagnetic charge. A cell does not eat; it is life-force energy that feeds it. Our cells are charged by the food we eat and the thoughts we think. Minerals found in fresh and raw vegetables and fruits act like magnets that hold solar energy. That is the main purpose of the food.

Basically, the same amount of food should come out that goes in, and the faster it is processed and eliminated the better your state of health will be. Food goes in, and the same amount comes out, unless it gets stuck to the colon walls. It is not the food itself but the energy within it that is used up. Plants don't "eat" soil either. The soil holds them and holds the moisture, but the plants eat energy (light). They pull the negative ions out of the earth and release them out through their leaves, and that charge alerts the neural hormones in our bodies when we eat them. Sprouts offer lots of pulsating life as well as many anticancer agents. Alfalfa plants, under certain conditions, have been known to penetrate their roots up to 150 feet into the earth to pull out healthy magnetic charges.

The Only Real Food Is Gratitude

When you eat your food, do so with tremendous awareness and gratitude. Just before you eat, expand your heart and let it feel the appreciation for that which is in front of you. Close your eyes and feel love and gratitude and thankfulness for your food and life. Let your eyes fill with real tears of thankfulness. This will transmute all things into right use. Eating will become a sacred, holy act. The food will become an elixir and the nectar of life if eaten this way. Everything you touch is then a holy communion.

Treat food as you would treat your friends — gently. When you eat, let your saliva say thank you. Whatever gratitude is heard inside echoes to the outside of the universe. Eat with such gratitude that it will fill you beyond measure. "More" is not needed when you eat like this. When you eat with gratitude you will heal your body slowly, quietly and appreciatively. It works. You eat less and less but your energy will be higher and higher.

Food is filled with pulsating life, energized by the sun. Eating less food results in living longer. If you eat slowly and consciously, you get full and won't need more. You become content, full and satisfied. Your taste buds resemble kernels of wheat and are symbolically the bread and wine of life. The holy marriage of communion with all life is built into your mouth. Your salivary glands, upon close examination, are even shaped like grapes. The sacredness is there, and you do not want to desecrate it.

Dietary habits change according to how you feel about yourself. Fresh raw vegetables and sprouts are alive and have high electromagnetic charges. When our thoughts are high and positive they, too, affect how we utilize and metabolize our food. The conscious person will never eat that which would jeopardize or destroy his body.

Keep the Body's Tissues Clean

We eat largely out of habit. When we eat too much, the cells build up debris. The same happens if our thoughts hold on to negative belief systems. Through experiments with frogs, researchers have learned that lactic acid, which is built up in tissues during movement, accounts for the stiffness that results from exercise. They've also discovered that if the tissues were cleansed with a saline solution, the frog could kick its legs indefinitely without exhaustion. We do not wear out when our tissues are clean. If there is unprocessed food locked up on the colon wall, this fecal matter often produces diverticulitis. These balloon-like protuberances from the colon walls hold toxins in. Let go of limiting beliefs of "I have to" or "I must" and the colon will let go. You eat less and get more out of it. If we feel we must hold onto life, we end up holding onto death rather than living.

Science has discovered that there is a metabolic rate of fixed energy. That means we all have an amount of calories that we can burn per pound of body weight before we die. It is surmised that humans can burn 80 million calories per pound of body weight. It is said that cats can burn enough calories to live about 20 years before they die, dogs around 12 years, and a mice three years. In the United States women live about 79 years and men about 72.5 years on average, and it appears that men typically take in more calories than women. Research has shown that there is a 60-70 percent increase in life span of mice by cutting the feedings by 50 percent.

Peter Duono, the Bulgarian Master, said that the stomach should never be filled; it should not be jammed to the limit. Always leave a space so your digestive juices can do their work.

Eating Reflects Our Thinking

People eat less when they are feeling emotionally secure and comfortable. When our thoughts are harmonious and we feel safe, we eat less. Whenever we think "survival" thoughts of any kind, they will trigger an eating response just as the first cold days of autumn trigger increased feeding in animals. The body swells to protect you from physical injury. If life feels threatening, you may swell up by adding on the pounds, even if it's only water retention. When we are uptight or feeling inadequate, we tend to need to eat more. When we are feeling more adequate and secure, we tend to eat less.

If you fear being hurt and you're very sensitive and don't want to feel pain or show your emotions, you will create a protective layer by gaining weight. Many sensitive people do this. Our thinking becomes a "mold" for us.

When metabolism is geared high and the temperature is turned up in the hypothalamus, we are revved up a little too high and may not be getting anywhere. Today's processed foods are so nutrient-depleted that consuming them can compel you to "graze" endlessly in search of sufficient nutrition. Relax, slow down, and don't worry so much. Metabolism is controlled by the mind. Do not emotionalize all the problems in life. Look at the problem without the emotion and work on the solution. Get the facts. Do not blame.

Vegetarianism

When an animal is killed, catabolism continues breaking down the complex molecules into simple ones. The flavorful taste of meat comes from the sudden release of waste products from the flesh of the animal's body. It is the waste in the tissues that gives meat its flavor; otherwise it would taste like bland plastic.

Eating fresh and raw plant life provides higher negative ion charges. When one eats this way, less food is required and less energy is needed for digestion; thus, more energy is acquired. Don't make vegetarianism a religion. Over time you are likely to be healthier and more clear-minded if you choose this style of eating. Carnivorous animals eat only vegetarian animals because the meat-eating animals are too toxic by virtue of their diet.

If you eat lots of cooked food as a main part of your diet, take digestive enzymes. Anything heated above 118-130 degrees F. will destroy the enzymes you must have in order to digest foods. Take these enzymes with anything that has been cooked or baked. In time, shift more to raw and fresh foods. Give yourself permission to eat what you want, but look at and listen to your body so it can tell you what is best for it. Drink fresh vegetable juices such as carrot, beet, celery, etc. Add to these several cloves of garlic. Make your juices fresh and never let them sit out for long or be stored. This type of eating will make for a healthy, clean colon and the body will be odor-free. No deodorant is needed when there is good body health.

Truly conscious people will never eat the kind of food that would jeopardize their lives.

QUESTIONS AND ANSWERS

A friend of ours asks this question, Peter. "Why do the foods that are the worst for you taste so good?'

I believe that on a subconscious level we all know exactly what the food will do to us or for us. Our tastes are a matter of unconscious conditioning. A simple example will suffice. When I was a teenager, another boy and I had gotten several big Cuban cigars. I suppose we thought this some rite of manhood. After the first few puffs, we were two sick puppies and green around the gills to boot. For years afterward just the hint of cigar smoke wafting on the air was enough to spasm my body.

As I said, our tastes are a matter of unconscious conditioning. The cigar smoke might remind someone else of a pleasant evening at home with their parents. But deeper still, under the surface layers, is an impulse for life or for death. Early experiences with issues of unworthiness, guilt and inferiority result in an unconscious urge toward death. This leads to the consumption of foods that will slowly deplete one of their life force and bring disease and death.

Even if, by sheer conscious will, you discipline yourself to eat only fresh and raw fruits and vegetables and drink the purest water, it will be in vain if you have not gotten deeply into the negative programming and its hidden unconscious messages. You can only do that after you get the band to stop marching in your head so you can hear the whispers inside your heart.

This chapter on "Food and Health" addresses a lot of emotional as well as physical issues. What about constipation? It appears that many people suffer from it. I'm sure there is a link between emotions, food intake and physical health. How does the mental state affect it?

If a person is not having one bowel movement for each meal consumed, from my viewpoint that person is constipated. I realize many readers will protest my position on this, but that is because their mental state is one of hanging on. When people operate their lives on the basis of addiction-backed demands and feel compulsively driven in the race to attain more sensations, more power and more security, there is often little time to relax. In a hectic world with busy schedules and constant demands, how can one expect to release the tension in the sphincter muscles enough to relax and evacuate? Does anyone comfortably and effectively empty their bowels while seated in a public bathroom, especially if it is between flights at an airport? Or how about in the morning when you are going to be late for work, or in a school between classes? What about the times there are a number of people waiting in line behind you? Consider how relaxed you feel if there is no door on the john. Anyone whose physical body is tight, tense and inflexible is constipated, though they may not admit it, of course. They think that those few rock-hard balls are normal, often not noticing the fat-laden floaters.

In my opinion, if the flesh of one's hand is not soft and resilient, if it does not bounce back immediately, one is too stiff, holding on, and thus constipated. All you need to do is hug someone to tell how constipated they are. Healthy flesh, healthy muscles, are resilient, soft when relaxed and yet retaining a firmness. The body must not feel like a sack of cement nor should the hands feel like hard, dead leather. The body on the other hand must not be like a loose bag of gel or pus. In either one of these two extremes, if the rubber band is stiff, hard and cracked, or limp and loose, you do not have enough muscle tone to move your bowels effectively enough for good health to result.

The remedy is to get on a good exercise program now! Even if you begin with just a morning walk, you must get the blood moving to those dying areas of stagnant flesh. Second, and more difficult, is to begin immediately to transform your emotionally charged addictions and panicky demands into mild preferences. How can you get uptight if what you prefer doesn't happen? But if it is a demand and it goes unfulfilled, isn't it just like a depth charge going off inside? Now try to have a healthy bowel movement!

From childhood, defecation has been associated with approval, but authentic approval from the outside world is impossible. Just consider for a moment the approval ratings you got from your parents when you failed to use the potty or messed your diapers. Proper evacuation of your bowels was always a measure of your goodness. Most folks were raised in environments of conditional love. That is, if you rake the yard, put your toys away, wash the dishes, you received conditional love and approval. So now the drama of how to perform in an acceptable manner so as to earn love is acted out. There is an "I must, but I can't!" conflict. Wow, what tension is built into this survival drama.

As an adult you launch into insane pursuits

and drive yourself to despair because even as a famous doctor, politician, or president of XYZ corporation, you still haven't earned the right to a good bowel movement. Ah, but if you were better looking, had a prettier wife, had a bigger car, finer home and a lot more money (and does a millionaire have enough money?), you could then relax!

I'll tell the story of a former mayor of a large city who called me on the phone. I heard strange noises through my receiver and asked him where he was. He said his call to me was the fortieth call that morning and so he took his mobile phone into the bathroom and was seated on the toilet. I told him it wasn't fair to talk with him under those conditions so I hung up on him. Some months later he died from cancer. He had been too busy looking for the world's approval to have a healthy bowel movement and thus filled up with poison and rotted with cancer from the inside out. It is always the same story.

All approval must be from inside out. All love must be first inside and then it can move outside. All healing must be from inside out.

People don't need doctors, they need masters. They need to first find out what a healthy person is supposed to look like and then ask them how they got that way; then, listen to the advice and apply it in their own lives. If you don't want to take responsibility for your own healing, then go to a doctor. If you accept total responsibility for your life, find out who has done the work, learn from them and go home and do the same.

What should a healthy bowel movement look like?

A great question. Most people have no idea. I'll give you a simple answer: if it is not green or orange and hasn't the consistency of peanut butter, you have a problem. One obviously does not have enough chlorophyll from fresh and raw foods if it is not green. If it is not orange, one hasn't had enough carrot juice. Simple, isn't it? Remember, green inside, clean inside!

What about the opposite of constipation, diarrhea?

Diarrhea is the body's way of expelling poisons in the fastest, most urgent manner possible. Odd that we medicate people to stop this from happening. It's very much the same as pulling the wires of the fire detector because it goes off in the middle of the night. What sane person would do that, and who would be so dumb as to go back to sleep? Isn't it better to go see what the problem is and seek a solution? Diarrhea is the alarm bell ringing to tell us there is too much poison in the body. Some might complain that after taking some herbs or juices they get diarrhea. Good! The body's warning system is still working and is allowing the herbs to kick the toxins out. Of course, on the other hand, you can drink and eat things you know are bad for you and overload the system and again the bell goes off.

There are people who have chronic diarrhea that lasts for years. The psychological aspect is that the person has been plagued by chronic fear of loss, or has recently gone through the loss of a lover or parent. Their feelings of impotency are overwhelming, and the poisoning effect of the negative emotions of loss result in not being able to contain their grief.

The same is true of people who only want to talk about their problems without exploring solutions. I once said to a person in the midst of such lamentations, "Whoa, please stop! I'm your friend, not a toilet, a garbage dump or trash can." This person was virtually clueless as to why they couldn't control their bowels. Those who cannot control their tongue cannot control their bowels. You would be very surprised at the intimate relationship between the mouth and tongue and the genitals and anus. What affects one affects the other. Obviously, what goes into the mouth comes out the anus — at least we hope so.

Also, the hands must be considered as they represent our life and its energy. If the hands tend to be weak, stiff or limp, that person has a weak grip on life — the result being mental and physical diarrhea. The cure is to take more control and responsibility for your individual life. It means making decisions and following through. It means taking commitment seriously.

You are only free to the degree that you have accepted responsibility for your life. This means you are in full control of your reality. When you are, then that insipid bumper sticker that has become so popular with diarrhea sufferers, "Shit happens," will no longer apply.

Would you speak to us about strength and diet?

There is a special breed of men whose thread of lineage weaves its way through antiquity and dwarfs the anti-effort mentality of today's weaklings and mental midgets. There was a special breed of men who loomed so large that they jumped out before us from the pages of history itself. These warrior sages of time stood so tall that emperors would beg permission to simply walk where their shadows had passed.

Self-confident, bold and forthright, the Greek Diogenes could intimidate Alexander the Great by his physical presence alone. Pythagoras, at one hundred years of age, would silence a gymnasium in Crotona filled with young wrestlers. His student Milo, one of the strongest men in history and wrestling champion of the 540 B.C. Olympics, was in steady awe of his teacher. Added to our list of vegetarian strongmen we cannot forget or leave out the strength of Samson or the power of Apollonius of Tyana.

You may be more familiar with a more recent golden era of strongmen and grapplers such as the Mighty Atom, Joe Greenstein, the eccentric Bernarr McFadden or the great wrestler and philosopher George Hackenschmidt, known as the Russian Lion.

Plato said, "When a beautiful soul harmonizes with a beautiful form and the two are cast in the same mold, that will be the fairest of sights to him who has an eye to see it." Emerson stated, "It is as easy for the strong to be strong as it is for the weak to be weak."

I say, why be content with the crumbs of weakness when you can drink the tonic of the strong? All the above-mentioned men had one factor in common: they all understood that this incredible machine we call the human body must have the finest and most natural fuel possible. They all endeavored to live and eat in harmony with nature. So what is the tonic of the strong and what does this special breed of man find to be the most strengthening and vitalizing foods to consume? In order to answer that question we must consider what nature has designed us to eat. Just what is the natural food for man?

If you noticed you had fangs and claws, would you not ask what these were to be used for, what is their intended purpose? If you noticed you could no longer grind food by moving your jaw in a lateral or sideways manner nor move your jaw forward or backward and were limited to an open-and-shut scissors-like bite, you could quickly conclude that you were designed for tearing, biting and swallowing food whole.

If, on further inspection of your mouth, you found fangs instead of thirty-two teeth composed of molars, incisors, cuspids and bicuspids, you could conclude that you were meant to be a carnivore. As a carnivore your saliva would have little effect on starches, unlike the saliva of a primate. Your tongue as a carnivore would be very rough, unlike the smooth tongue of an ape, and you would be reduced to drinking by lap-

ping instead of by suction like an ape, nor would you any longer perspire like a human or an ape. And if your fingernails grew into claws, you would be correct in concluding that your natural food would be raw meat.

Now you want to object and protest that it tastes so good and makes you so strong? There is a special breed of men who would turn their faces from you in disdain and disbelief that your appetite is stronger than your will. Or is it that the power of reason has disappeared?

You may retort, "Look at how strong a meat-eating lion or tiger is." I would reply, "Look at a bull, an elephant, a rhino, a bear or a gorilla." How is it that nature allows them to turn grass into muscle? Consider, for instance, the fruitarian chimpanzee. The chimp is at least eight times stronger than a man, and we cannot even begin to draw a comparison of strength with a gorilla.

Put a gorilla into the octagon of the Ultimate Fighting Championships, and the gorilla, in a heartbeat, would bend the largest, most skillful steroid monster into a pathetic pretzel without drawing a drop of sweat. As a matter of fact, the chimp would do the same thing.

The men of old would frown in disgust at such weaklings and admonish us all to go back to nature. Go back to our natural diet, and then we, too, would regain our strength, health and original life span, which, by the way, isn't three score and ten. That's the one assigned to wimps.

I admit that there are some very strong men out there, but how much stronger would they be if they chose the diet that nature chose for us? Don't you consider it sad that so many of these meat-eating strongmen die so young? Oh, you don't believe it? Then you haven't been reading the right magazines. Just read Sons of Samson by David Webster. Webster profiles every great strongman he could find data on. As I turned the pages of this fascinating book, I was shocked at the very young ages at which these men died. They were ignorant of nature's diet.

The wisdom of Solomon echoes in my ears: "It is better to be a live dog than a dead lion." I say it is better to be a living Diogenes or a Pythagoras, and if you have the misfortune of dying, then at least be the one who rules in the Halls of Valhalla. Doesn't it make sense to endeavor to be as young, as healthy and as strong as long as you can? We are not designed to be shooting stars. We are designed to be shining stars, allowing our light to shine from whatever mountaintop we choose to climb.

There is no shortcut to strength and health. It is a narrow path, a royal road that leads to authentic health and unbelievable strength, and few are finding it. Broad and spacious is the path of foolish drugs, eat-anything diets and nutritional supplements made of coal tar and sewage sludge. They all lead to destruction.

Could you further expand on physical strength? Your feats have been recorded in several publications and on video.

First, there is the vehicle and then there is the driver. If you are driving a tractor, you'll not be geared like a race car even if the person on the tractor has previously driven race cars (the tractor is the body and the driver is the mind). The physical unit is one thing and the mental unit is another. It is the spirit or degree of the intensity of the life force that is the prime mover of the mind, which in turn sends electrochemical signals to the endocrine system and allows for the release of a vast array of responses. Adrenaline, for example, can be a "super octane" when released in sufficient quantity. Our emotional response can release very powerful neuropeptides, some even 50 to 100 times more powerful than morphine — and that makes us impervious to physical pain. Consider the effect when coupled with a dose of strength-enhancing adrenaline.

We have all heard the accounts of frail, little old ladies lifting cars off of someone in an acute emergency. I often repeat the story as reported by the Associated Press of a 53-year-old heart patient lifting a 1,800 lb. pipe off a little six-year-old boy who was being crushed by it near a construction site. The list goes on and on of these types of incredible feats. It is quite obvious that when the emotional state is peaked, great strength can be released.

Imagine a person who is in control of his thoughts and emotions, a person who can block out distractions and focus with laser-like con-

centration on the task at hand. This person can consciously supply their vehicle with rocket fuel — but they had better make certain all the nuts and bolts will hold so they don't blow their engine up! Of course, this is really not a cause for concern since what is required for such conscious control of the mind is that a person has mastered the body. By that I mean, mastered simple things such as appetite and bad dietary habits. That person is the epitome of self-control, and the condition of their physical body shows it.

That's why a person who has truly mastered his mind will always have a perfected body as evidence. Don't be misled — fat and obese people parading around as masters are walking contradictions. Master your mind and not even be able to muster enough self-control to conquer your appetite? Nonsense! On the other hand, this doesn't mean one has to have large, bulging muscles. You may or may not. What's important is that you're not too fat or too thin.

Health is the middle path. Buddha's example is perfect. After going to extremes in the direction of physical thinness and teaching the middle way, who could ever believe he would show such lack of self-control, such lack of mastery over his appetite, as to end up like the fat Buddha statues we see? One must understand that in a nation where famine is a regular occurrence, fatness is seen as richness. For example, a fat cow was better than a skinny one. Thus, hungry people want to portray their spiritual teacher as fulfilled and spiritually rich. So, a skinny statue won't do. As a side note, China portrays the Buddha as thinner and Japan as fatter; yet, Buddha never authorized any statues of himself to be made.

Now, back to physical strength. How do we build a strong physical vehicle? As it must be apparent to you by now, it must occur from the inside out. Control the mind and you will control the body. As to the physical chemicals involved, and there are too many to inject into this conversation, the main ingredient of muscle construction and growth is testosterone.

For the ultimate extension of life span, you must lower your core body temperature; increase negative ions; avoid the increase of the excessive production of the death hormone, serotonin;

and control your metabolic rate of fixed energy which means a lower caloric intake per pound of muscles mass. You must also bolster and guard against immune system failure and eliminate cross-linking and free radical damage to body tissues. Also, go far beyond the Hayflick limit for cell replication, and last, but extremely important, correct any sexual dysfunction.

How can anyone control his mind and yet not be able to control his sexual urge? Pythagoras taught that the loss of semen weakens the brain. Semen is rich in an organic phosphorized fat called lecithin which is what brain and nerve tissue is made from. Just consider one of Pythagoras' students, Milo. Milo the Pythagorean was one of the strongest men in history. He lived strictly on a raw food diet and ate no meat. He also was said to be a chaste man as were the famous Spartans who were both feared and renowned in all the ancient world.

In the early 1920's much research was conducted on the connection between testicular extracts, glands and rejuvenation and physical strength. One researcher, an experimental physi-

ologist named Dr. Voronoff, transplanted new sex glands into castrated rams and oxen. These animals were chosen because of the dramatic, observable changes that take place in the bodies of castrated rams and oxen: the heads change shape and become very narrow and long, the bodies lose muscle and gain fat tissue instead, bones elongate, and horns stop growing and assume the shape of the horns of females. But when new sex glands were transplanted into the old castrated rams and oxen, new muscle suddenly appeared, fat melted instantly, and their horns grew large and powerful. The bone structure of their heads even changed.

One famous experiment that Voronoff performed in 1920 was on a decrepit 70-year-old man. Voronoff transplanted monkey testicles into him. For three years the man was young again, living a full, active life. His muscles had even rejuvenated and his face was different. But, even though it lasted only three years, Voronoff was convinced he had discovered an important key to health and strength.

There were many other pioneers as well. Drs. Lorand, Steinach, Brown-Sequard and

Brinkley to name a few. The message is a time-honored one that resonates through the halls of antiquity. Testosterone and its conservation builds health and strength beyond description. It is that which fuels and powers and transforms the physical machine, and it is the amazing, powerful force of life found in semen. When used properly it can create a superman, or used improperly create an unempowered creepling. The choice is always before us. The way of the sage or the way of the world.

What about females?

It is the same. Keep the glands and organs healthy. Practice conservation and a powerful, beautiful goddess will be the result, not some bloated image popularly portrayed today in statue form as "the Goddess," but rather a beautiful form reminiscent of the statues of ancient Greece in her glory days.

Would you briefly tell us about your diet and health?

Certainly. I am on a "gorilla diet" of fresh and raw herbs, fruits and veggies. I am never sick, never have a cold or any other disease that afflicts the masses, and I never go to doctors. Why should I? If I want to ask the doctors anything, I'll find them seated in my audiences.

What is a "Merrwe Wabbit," Peter? How often and how many ounces a day do you suggest we drink? How much do you and Ann consume?

A "Merrwe Wabbit" began as a humorous take-off on an alcoholic drink called a "Bloody Mary," which is basically vodka and tomato juice. I suggested turning the "Bloody Mary" into a health drink for those who didn't care for raw carrot juice and who enjoyed an alcoholic beverage. I must emphatically state, this is what I do, and the results I receive are obvious. This drink that I am about to describe is NOT — *I repeat,* NOT — *for mortals. If you insist on trying it, go get permission from your doctor, dentist, mortician, mommy, daddy and big brother. In other words: This is a disclaimer.*

I firmly believe that if you are sick, you will never get well without a juicer. As for Ann and myself, there is almost never a day that passes in which we do not consume, at minimum, a quart of raw vegetable juice each.

First ingredient: organic carrot juice. Norman Walker states in his book, Raw Vegetable Juices: *"One pint of carrot juice daily has more constructive body value than twenty-five pounds of calcium tablets." It cleans the liver and is one of the most powerful natural solvents for cancer and ulcers. Examine the molecules of carrot juice, and you will find them to have almost exactly the same form as a blood molecule. I could write a book extolling the virtues of carrot juice.*

Secondly, I drop into the juicer a very hot *cayenne pepper. Herbalist Dr. Richard Schulze states in the book by Sam Biser,* Curing with Cayenne, *"If you master only* one *herb in your life, master cayenne pepper. It is more powerful than any other. You can normalize blood pressure in three months with garlic, but when you add enough cayenne, it can happen in three days." I might add that you will never have a heart problem again. Cayenne's acrid and biting properties, in both its oil and resin, can be completely extracted when mixed in alcohol. It is a powerful stimulant, and it is guaranteed to light your fire!*

Next comes garlic. It is so powerful that in areas of Russia where there were no doctors it earned the nickname of "Russian penicillin." It is so penetrating and potent that it will almost instantly dissolve and clear the mucus from the lungs, bronchial tubes and sinus cavities. With garlic you'll never have worms, parasites, asthma, TB or high blood pressure. Ann and I consume a bulb — not a clove — between us almost every day. Four to six small cloves go into the "Merrwe Wabbit."

Next, we put in a whole lime and a whole lemon, peel and all (be sure to wash and brush peel thoroughly first). The skins are an incredibly rich source of bioflavonoids. You can, in just a few days' time, rid yourself of kidney stones and gallstones just by the juice of one lemon in hot water supplemented with carrot and cucumber juice. Also, lemon juice and extra-vir-

gin, cold-pressed olive oil is a classic liver and gallbladder cleanser.

Parsley is the next juicing ingredient. Parsley is essential to the health of the thyroid and adrenal glands as well as for the urinary tract, bladder and kidneys. It will also relieve menstrual cramps. It is essential for oxygen metabolism.

Ann and I also add horseradish and comfrey when they are available and fresh.

Next, we add a little alcohol in the form of vodka. The alcohol is a carrier that immediately transports these fabulous nutrients into the bloodstream and through the body. If you have never had a "Merrwe Wabbit," you will be surprised at the powerful warmth the cayenne pepper and alcohol have on the entire circulatory system. Just imagine all the capillaries and arteries expanding and being cleansed.

Many people are very opposed to the use of alcohol. Social convention or religious bias is a very powerful, corrosive fear. If you are a recovering alcoholic, I do not *recommend this ingredient. However, since you asked what* I *do, I have included it. Our bodies have special enzymes that metabolize one ounce or so of pure alcohol that our bodies naturally produce. That's the same as forty ounces of beer or twenty ounces of wine — per day! Raw, unfiltered, organic apple cider vinegar with the mother ("mother of vinegar" occurs naturally as strand-like chains of connected protein molecules) can be substituted for the vodka.*

The danger is not the alcohol itself; it is when it is converted by the enzyme alcohol dehydrogenase into acetaldehyde. This is a cousin of formaldehyde, the product used to tan leather and embalm bodies. Thankfully, our body has another enzyme, aldehyde dehydrogenase, which oxidizes the toxic acetaldehyde into a harmless vinegar to be excreted through the bloodstream.

Since most people eat nothing but cooked and processed foods devoid of enzymes, it is no wonder alcohol is so devastating. Once you heat even an organic fresh veggie to 118-130 degrees Fahrenheit, you have destroyed all the enzymes in the food and, thus, overtax the pancreas to keep up with the loss of enzymes. Ann and I don't have this problem.

Now that you have the ingredients all mixed together with a shot of vodka, taste and tone down its heat slightly by adding fresh tomato juice. Add ice, sprinkle a little minced, dry onion on top, and enjoy this health extravaganza.

Oh yes! We drink two each evening. That's sixteen ounces each. We enjoy them along with a plate of raw veggies to dip and snack on. That is dinner.

Our main meal of the day is a fresh salad with olive oil and apple cider vinegar with the mother in it as a dressing. We enjoy that in the afternoon.

Health and Sexuality

Replenish the Body's Nutrients

Sexual activity is rewarding and enriching, but also physiologically taxing. Sexuality is the seed of life. When the seed is always going out, the body may become deficient in certain substances. This is why it is particularly important for males to have sufficient amounts of calcium, magnesium, zinc and lecithin. Pure ginseng helps maintain sexual youth in the male. Sarsaparilla and saw palmetto also help. These herbs help foster rejuvenation and longevity by strengthening the body functions which can be weakened by the release of sexual fluids.

The prostate is often overtaxed if there is insufficient zinc available, increasing the likelihood of prostate cancer. The foods we eat affect our sexual energy. The ingestion of protein makes one more sexual. Long-distance runners and those who frequently fast have decreased sexual drives.

When sexual fluid is kept in the body, certain rejuvenation occurs. Men with vasectomies, where the vas deferens is cut and the sperm stays in the body, will often experience rejuvenation. When the sperm is retained, the life force is kept inside. One advantage of a vasectomy for a male is that many of the key fluids are kept within the body. This allows a rest for the adrenals. There is a mystical metaphysical force of life within us and we can waste it or we can use it for creativity.

Be Moderate In Sexuality

People are sometimes obsessed with sex because they sense an unsettledness in the world and worry that they will be dead at an early age. Their root chakras become overstimulated. A lot of AIDS develops out of root-chakra stimulation — a fear of not living or feeling unsettled.

If you have sex every night, it's the same as having pizza every night. It no longer is so tasty, and you begin to look for new ways to stimulate the drive.

Sexual activity is highly electrical and draws vital life force from us. Rejuvenation of the body is possible when one is not overly active sexually. Conservation of sexual energy results in more for the body to work with in terms of minerals. Too much sex may not allow the phosphorus loss to be replaced quickly enough and can cause calcium loss, both of which contribute to the weakening of mental functions and concentration, and to bone breakage.

Often there is a transmutation of sexual energy that doesn't occur until the late forties or into the fifties. This is when the sexual energy is transmuted into particular talents, such as art, music or speaking. This is why so many people are not well known until their late forties or early fifties. The conserved sexual energy can then be focused on other goals.

Rejuvenation of the body is possible when one is not overly active sexually.

QUESTIONS AND ANSWERS

Peter, a friend has a question regarding the physical losses that you say occur with sexual activity. She asks, "Does love change the physical losses? Is sexual activity more depleting without love than with love?"

Yes, and I commend you on the question. Now, I have a question: Why would one have sexual activity with someone he does not love? I suppose the world has been working on that one for thousands of years. Perhaps it's the same reason people scratch an itch.

Peter, would you talk a little more about women's health issues?

Certainly. However, I must point out that all health issues have the same origin. Health is an issue of internal and external hygiene and not an issue of gender, for even gender can be changed by hormonal alteration.

Breast cancer strikes men as well as women, yet we are conditioned to view it as solely a fem-

inine malady. I have stressed the importance of the male's conservation of seminal fluids, but the female must also guard against the losses of sexual secretions by the oviducts, ovaries and uterus, which acts as a seminal receptacle. Fluids and secretions are lymphatically drawn and collected at the thoracic duct as chyle and eventually fed to the heart and blood. There is a very powerful relationship between the lymphatic, nervous and vascular systems and the genital glands.

I find it interesting that the sex glands are the only endocrine glands that can lose their fluids through secretion. The myelin sheath which covers the nerves is constructed chiefly of lecithin, the main ingredient of the endocrine sex-gland fluid. Its loss leads to a lowering of brain-building stimulation. A normal brain is somewhere around 28 percent lecithin and the brains of the insane, 14 percent. Men and women with high sexual-fluid losses begin to lose control of emotions and self-control.

Consider the behavioral abnormalities that may occur at the time a female menstruates, or during her so-called change of life, menopause.

It is claimed that menstruation is triggered by a monthly, cyclical rise in blood pressure. But there would be no menstruation/bleeding if there were no catarrh inflammation from uric acid and the congestion of minute capillaries by toxic blood and mucous, clogging the mucous membranes of the uterus. I concur with many health purists who agree that a menstruating uterus is a diseased uterus.

The best way to reduce inflammation and irritation of the mucous membranes is to alkalize the body by a diet of fresh and raw fruits and vegetables and by eliminating mucous-forming, acid-building foods such as eggs, dairy products and meat from one's diet. Consider that adult female primates in the wild do not menstruate. In captivity, menstruation follows a change in diet.

Many women have asked what they can do about candida. These women have noticed a lack of concentration, difficulty with control of emotions, nervousness, digestive disorders, diarrhea and constipation. The answer is the same — internal and external hygiene. No matter how many names medical people find for disease, there is only one disease: pollution of the body by accumulated waste. And nature provides the remedy, a natural raw food diet, pure water, fresh air, sunshine and fasting.

Once I suggested hydrotherapy, a douche, for a woman with candida. She was shocked and replied, "I would never put anything like that in there!" And I was shocked to think that a woman would not wash inside. I knew another woman who called me for help after being raped who never considered using a douche for hours afterward. By not douching, it did help prove she was sexually attacked, but it also showed our culture's general lack of hygienic awareness. There is every indication that a large segment of our population is debased and diseased by constantly seeking new sensations while never cleansing the past abuses of both mind and body.

Many women complain of not being able to get pregnant, though personally I would question why any woman would want to at this time in history. We are bombarded with all types of sexual inducements, and men tend to boast of sexual performance, genital size and sexual conquests. These types of issues led me to conclude many years ago that the world has its head screwed on backwards. And now we have a new performance drug, Viagra, which I suppose will be obsolete by the time this interview is published, only to be replaced by another drug that helps men impregnate women and continue spinning the world's "merry-go-round" until it grinds down into a "sorry-go-round."

People who engage in frequent sexual intercourse with exchange of fluids are unaware that absorbed semen has a very harmful effect on the ovaries and the female's blood. It acts as a foreign protein that can cause sterility and, if pregnancy ensues, may alter the brain growth of the embryo. The female may develop a "spermatotoxin," which is a common occurrence among prostitutes and frequently results in sterility.

When one considers that the purity of the womb is the forecast of the future, one might also recall the old biblical text that reminds us, "The life of the soul is in the blood."

As far as every health and social issue goes,

clean the blood and that pure river of life will cleanse the world in purity and in light.

Can one go so far in eating healthy foods that sexual desire and creativity both decrease?

Eating healthy foods results in health — period! Now, as far as the question is concerned, you can create on the outside or in the inside. You can be involved with creating families or philosophies. Why be so concerned with sexual desire? You'll get the itch and sneeze again. No need to worry. And if you don't....

You can fast and exercise until there is no more available energy. Then both sex and creativity are gone. When a fruit tree is deprived of water, sun and compost, it will not have the energy to bear fruit. A flower is fragrant only because of an abundant energy. Energy is life and life is creative. The flower has no choice as to the channel for its life force. We do.

People who are consumed by sexual desire should consider if it is or is not the physical body's last cry for help before death knocks at their door. You have heard the saying "I'm too sick to die!" Just before death there is a sudden, last-ditch bolt of energy. Since sex is survival for the species, sex and death are connected. Often in sick people, sexual desire is a pleading for life. Sex in its natural manner is designed to allow life to go on by replicating humans. The sex drive in spiritually motivated people is, for the most part, transmutated or sublimated to the creation of an inner being. The energy is needed for our rebirth, our flowering, our spiritual fragrance.

So is sex wrong? Of course not. Sex is an energy and how you use it is up to you. But since you have asked... yes, there are foods that will increase desire and decrease desire. That's why in certain religious cultures certain foods are taboo and long fasts are imposed. Look at the dilemma in a monastic order when energy and desire mix. And may God save the choirboys.

Now bear in mind the world of nature: When an animal ceases to be able to bear offspring, it begins to die. When a fruit tree can no longer bear fruit, it has started its descent. When sexual desire dies in a human, twenty, maybe even thirty years are left. Do not misunderstand me: I said simply desire, a purely biological drive. Concupiscence is our natural healthy state. This energy state is a rich boon both physically and spiritually. In the scriptures Jesus refers to the body of Christ as a bride adorned for her husband. This chaste bride, made of many members, has saved and conserved her creativity and desires and applied them in a higher direction. So may we all die to that which is beggarly and lowly and ascend to the fruitage of the divine which is noble and high, for in it shall we be blessed by that which no man may speak, by that which is a vision eternal.

In our modern times people tend to experiment with the full ranges of sexual expression. Would you care to comment?

My focus is on what works in developing the seed of human potential and its resultant flowering. I'll leave the moral judgments to the clergy and other guilt-ridden deviates. What concerns me is how greater purity, greater luminosi-

ty, greater clarity can be attained. While living in the fleshly house, as I've said before, there are laws of convention and laws of nature. The laws of convention change with society and culture; the laws of nature never change.

I will comment on one base practice, anal copulation. That's not a pun. Consider how in order for a male to impregnate a female, at least one seed must survive. The law of nature fills semen with immune-cell inhibitors. That means the immune system is impotent in dealing with semen. What do you think takes place when semen is injected into a person? It is like a rectal implant. In anal copulation, it is just like injecting an immune-cell inhibitor directly into the bloodstream. If the semen carries a virus, it will be able to offer strong resistance to the body's immune cells and their ability to destroy the infection. This practice is more dangerous than playing a game of Russian roulette with a loaded revolver up your butt. It all depends on how suicidal one is as to how much fun is returned. Hey, if that's sexual expression, who am I to interfere? After all, consider the population explosion.

If one's interest has gone from fun to fulfillment, then I am certain to be of some help. Modern times can have no effect on time-honored wisdom — there is great suffering everywhere and there is also a way out of that suffering. Everything we see with our eyes or hear with our ears, everything we touch with our hands and taste with our mouths is transitory. As the great master is reported to have said, "Seek not what rust can consume, what thieves can steal or moths devour. Seek first the Kingdom and its righteousness (right-use-ness) and all these other things shall be added to you."

How vital, how crucial it is that we seek not the things of the world, the showy display of one's means, the desire of the eyes and so on. We must seek with all our heart, all our strength and all our mind the Kingdom of consciousness and its right-use-ness. It is an arduous path, cramped and narrow, with few finding the way to that which does not die, to that which is eternal, to that which fills the heart and brightens the soul. If you ask if I would teach health, I will teach spirit, and if you ask for me to point the way, I will take your hand in mine and walk. If you ask for light, I will show you the very sun itself!

There are people who would suggest using a condom to address some of the concerns you mention above. Would you care to comment?

My teaching and message have nothing to do with endorsing one's method of suicide, nothing to do with patronizing pleasure addicts, nothing to do with pitiful creatures whose sole ambition in life is to intensify immediate gratification. If their sole ambition is to find more bizarre ways of satisfying their itch, they should seek those who can instruct them. You'll find them in lower astral hells where everyone has a pain in the ass.

I am here to lead one out of that place, out to a more fulfilling and luminous life. I am here to call one out from the world of dust to the world of spirit, out from the world of addictions into the bright world of personal power, out from slavery into freedom. How will they hear the call if the message is not sharp and clear? If I am not bold, I am bound to be misunderstood. Many will miss and be offended by my words, and unfortunately few have their heart and mind open enough to listen. In all candor, I must say that if one has concluded that the zenith of human experience is finding something to stick up their ass, excuse me while I make my exit!

However, if one has already concluded that there is no amount of satiation of the senses that can bring an end to suffering, an end to despair, an end to frustration, and that one is willing to drop the bag of burden and appetite, then I am ready to show the way that I have traveled the path to the summit. There will be those who misunderstand me, thinking I preach renunciation, when in fact I teach simply dropping a lesser pleasure for a greater and more everlasting joy!

If that doesn't interest you, just consider the numerous studies done on prostatic hyperplasia and prostate cancer. In one study done on men with an average age of sixty-three years, forty-six percent of the study group had organ-confined prostate cancer. In another study, eighty percent of eighty-year-old men had prostate cancer. When did it start? It was developing for many years before being detected. How many men in their forties are already discovering they have difficulty in controlling their bladder, or that they have that subtle, unexplainable pain, or that they need to urinate and can only dribble? Consider also that prostate cancer is often growing on the outside of the gland and gives no warning sign until it is too late.

Here is the point. If a penis, or something like a penis, is inserted into the anus on a regular basis, causing an unnatural stimulation of a gland that may or may not be in the process of hyperplasia or tumor growth and irritating it with regularity, the recipient will have slightly better than a fifty percent chance of dying from prostate cancer. Go ahead and tell me you are not playing Russian roulette — even if you stretched a condom over the barrel. If this doesn't make any sense to you, there is no need to read further. But for some, this single sheet of paper may be what saves their lives.

Peter, sometimes I feel that your answers will be shocking to our readers. People are unaccustomed to such graphic bluntness. Maybe you should go softer.

One can always be tender and soft with a person who has awakened. I agree, it is shocking to have someone break an ammonia capsule under your nose to revive you from an unconscious state. It is shocking to have CPR performed on you when you have been pulled out of the ocean and almost drowned. If your house were ablaze, would you want someone to softly whisper in your ear a warning as you continued to sleep, or would it not be better to be shocked out of your stupor?

Those people who know me more intimately experience my softness. It is certainly against my nature to be rough with others. If I made the mistake of judging myself according to the interpretation of others of what and how I say things, I would indeed be sad; but I am too centered within myself for that to be the case. I have lived long enough to consider conclusions regarding those topics. That is perhaps what is actually shocking. In a world of "whatever you say," where politically indecisive people float around as wandering generalities, never making a concrete statement about anything, a deliberate, purposeful individual is indeed a shock.

I am not saying my opinions or my conclusions are always perfectly accurate, but they are mine, and they are formed by reason coupled with consciousness. I always stand to be corrected when new facts come to light on any subject. I will always bow before truth.

What should one do when one has discovered one great truth or many truths? Should it be hidden under a bushel basket, smothered by soft platitudes, hidden in a linguistic fog, or set boldly upon the mountaintop for all to see? I don't like shouting from the rooftop, and yet, in a flood of irrationality and ignorance, what other method is effective?

I would rather spend my time writing poems of love; yet how can I shut my mouth after countless people have come with tear-stained cheeks and eyes full of gratitude, begging me to say it again? "Please, Peter, say it louder..." In the days to come, many will be glad I did.

The Effects of Environment on Your Health

The Full Moon and the Charge of the Ionosphere

Why is it that many people feel a little touch of lunacy during a full moon? It is because of an increase in positive ions. An ion is an atom that has lost or gained an electron. Electrons are very fickle due to being eighteen hundred times lighter than protons, so you can see how easily they can slip away from an atom.

The earth has a negative ion charge. From the earth to the edge of the ionosphere is a distance of approximately twenty-five to two hundred fifty miles. At the bottom of this layer of highly charged particles, those closest to the earth have the heaviest positively charged ions. The negative ion charges lie at the upper levels of the ionosphere, beyond the earth's surface. The moon also has a negative ion charge. When the full moon in its elliptical orbit is closest to the earth (each month the distance from the earth varies between 221,000 and 253,000 miles), its negative ion charge and the upper negatively-charged ionosphere repel each other just as two magnets do when you place similar poles together. This pushes the positively charged ions of the ionosphere down to the earth.

This positive charge causes our bodies to produce greater amounts of the neurohormone serotonin. Serotonin is a smooth-muscle stimulator and stimulates especially the heart and central nervous system. Excessive amounts of serotonin can cause copious amounts of bleeding, depression, and high blood pressure. It can trigger an overproduction of histamines that can cause allergies to flare up and make you think you have a cold.

Eighty percent of excessive bleeding occurs during the full moon. Often surgeries are postponed at these times. There is frequently more edginess and greater pain experienced during this phase of the moon.

Connecting with Earth Energy

If we live in an environment with large amounts of concrete and steel, we will have fewer negative ions because of a lack of contact with the earth. In that type of an environment our nervous system is especially affected. The dendrites, the branched parts of a nerve cell that carry impulses toward the cell body, have a tendency to shrivel and atrophy. Those who work in concrete buildings with air conditioning and no open windows are insulated from the relaxing negative ion sources. Big cities usually have plenty of positive ions and very little earth energy. Because of this they are largely geographical insanity centers. Living full-time in large cities doesn't allow for much "grounding" or stimulation from the earth. So if you live in one, have a place to raise flowers, take walks in the park, or simply be outside in a natural environment daily.

Also seriously consider purchasing a negative-ion generator. The newer and more powerful models can produce an effect similar to standing by a waterfall. These can be placed in a sleeping room or room where you work much of the day. Utilizing water can also be helpful when the aura "gets sticky" from electromagnetic pollution. Pure water cleanses and washes away the positive ion charge.

Waterbeds are not recommended. They pull in energy and hold onto it just like a battery. Do not sleep in waterbeds that others have slept in because their emotional charge is there. At times, a waterbed will collect primarily positive charges, the result being that the person awakens drained of energy and edgy.

You have to relax and get your environment under control because stress causes most of our health problems. A toxic, electromagnetically unbalanced environment is poisonous.

Minimize Contact with Major Electrical Lines

All electrical appliances give off electromagnetic pollution and emit positive ions that are not good for health. Some people use Pulsors™ near or on electrical equipment. These Pulsors™ pull the electricity into themselves. You can also use a tic tracer to find out how much electrical pollution is given off from any given appliance or piece of equipment. Tic tracers can be purchased from

Radio Shack or a similar kind of store. Wearing biomagnetic bracelets or necklaces has been reported to have a favorable effect.

We Are Rainbows of Sound and Fragrance

Keep your personal environment clean. Fragrant scents are natural to a physically and spiritually cleansed person who chooses to live in a pure environment. These people have a natural fragrance and positive scent and do not require a deodorant. People are pure when their minds are continuously nourished with wholesome thoughts — when they choose to be mentally operational.

The sages of old were known to have fragrantly characteristic scents. They could be detected even when the sage could not be seen because of their dominant energy characteristic.

Be As Beautiful on the Inside As on the Outside

What shows as beauty on the outside must have inner purity for true beauty to exist.

Once Peter visited a beautiful mission church in southern Arizona, he found it to be beautiful on the outside, but he became absolutely nauseous as he detected the smell of death and anguish that had penetrated the pictures and walls inside. He realized there had been Native Americans who were forced to build the mission and whose bones were buried underneath and utilized as part of the foundation.

Keep About You Only Those Things Which Feel Right

Consider that which is in your own home and surroundings. What do the old photographs and paintings on the wall tell you? What is your gut-level reaction to what you see? Even with inheritances, be sure they are right for you. Watch out for inherited jewelry, old articles of clothing and particularly old religious artifacts. Do they have positive meaning, memory and energy for you? Throw away that which does not work rather than hoarding the past.

Perhaps a house you inherit isn't right for you but would be for someone else. Money obtained from the sale of an inherited home is readily exchangeable and can be circulated positively or invested. You cannot go back and recreate your past by living in the old home. Let someone else live there who would be grateful.

Recirculate things. Money is energy. If tainted, spend it or use it proactively in a practical way. It is how we feel about things. There is no sense in feeling guilt about receiving an inheritance. Consider the fact that when you die you have to leave it to someone. Certain sentimental items may be of value if they hold warm emotions and feelings. If they are gloomy, get rid of them. Take the inheritance and make something good from it.

Art, Color and Music

Certain music can rejuvenate and heal. The same is true with colors. Colors and their vibrations are very important.

Have you ever noticed how, in our various moods, we choose to wear certain colors? There are no bad colors but since all colors have a vibration, they will make us feel a certain way. Be sure to wear colors that make you feel good. Wearing whites and lighter colors will often make you feel calmer and lighter. Wearing black may be the color of choice for a funeral, but why make it your attire in everyday life unless your whole life is a funeral procession? You may consider what color your face turns when you are angry. Could it be that if you wear red you experience angry emotions more? You might experiment and find out.

You will also be attracted to different types of music based on how you are feeling. We are conditioned by the music we hear, so determine what you want to feel and choose the music that produces those results. Certain sounds open up various glands in the body and secretions of adrenaline or of endorphins occur. Our glandular system is provoked by sound vibrations. A drumbeat can take you into a hypnotic state.

Music can open you up and make you vibrantly alive. To grow and evolve, pay close attention to the music you listen to daily and why you like it. Glandular secretions create changes in the body, even altering its shape.

If you read Peter's accounts in The Luminous Life, *you'll be stunned at the healing possibilities of color, music and scent.*

Certain rock music withers plants. Certain classical music promotes growth. Plants will even wrap themselves around and embrace the speakers. Beinsa Douno, a Bulgarian Master, was able to clear out an entire bar filled with rowdy patrons when he wanted to, just by playing his violin. The room he rented was above a bar, and when he had enough of the noise below, he played his music. It was so healing on a deep energy level that the people left. It was too much for them.

Art and music should bring out your highest. Art can be a celebration of the human spirit. Affirmations in music must never be negative or harsh. Make your home and office light and airy. Place pictures and paintings that are beautiful and pure in your environment. Do not have art that looks like graffiti.

This world is heaven on earth when we see beauty in it.

QUESTIONS AND ANSWERS

I'm going to ask a rather neutral question: What music do you recommend listening to?

Anything that has a positive effect. Watch out for the lyrics. I personally enjoy music with a largo tempo. That's music in the area of 64 beats per minute; somewhat like a heartbeat. It's very meditative.

Longevity and Immortality

Our Thoughts Age or Rejuvenate Us

If you enjoy life and it is fulfilling for you, you will stay alive as long as you want to. Celebrate your rarity; you are who you are. Let your body vibrate with luminous life and health. The body will follow luminous thoughts like an obedient servant. These thoughts keep you useful in life and as long as you have purpose, you will continue to live abundantly. Immortality just may be possible.

You can stay as long as life is pleasurable. This pleasure response is triggered in the brain when you are achieving fulfillment and are excited. At these times of satisfaction, endorphins are produced, physical levels of pain decrease and our levels of contentment soar.

If life is not joyful and fulfilling, be prepared to leave this world. Our attitude makes all the difference. Humans cultivate philosophies of usefulness or they start to die.

We age by our thoughts, especially worry. A good thought strengthens and rejuvenates. Confused thinking and the anxieties of the "what ifs" hold us back and will wear out the system quickly and age us on all cellular levels. Aging occurs when our DNA can't give forth its messages. If DNA holds on, it is called cross-linking, and the cell dies. Two strands of sugar and phosphate molecules form the DNA double helix containing our genetic code. If they reach across the gap and share a hydrogen bond, they have cross-linked, or grabbed hands. For the DNA to be functional and replicate itself it must "let go" — otherwise the structure dies.

DNA repair is greatly influenced by our mental attitudes: Let go and live. Our thoughts are as important as the food we ingest. Thoughts activate the glands. Glandular production can make us more youthful, or it can age us.

In Order to Stay Alive, Love This Life With Passion... In the Moment

The person who is focused and loves life stays alive. When people are confused, there is a problem, and the mind will not direct the immune system adequately.

AIDS is born of fear and confusion. AIDS is aptly named as it is a statement of "help me," or "aid me." One needs to direct one's thoughts. If there is a cancer involved, then command the macrophages to gobble up the cancer cells. An immune system is often more "alert" in persons who are opinionated because they are so decisive. Do not think about illness. Focus on absolute health. Take time to explore issues for certainty.

Some don't believe in the aging and dying process. They are indeed radical thinkers. Some who embrace the juice of life and who pursue living believe in physical as well as spiritual immortality. Of course, the proof must be observable. There is a story about a man who didn't know he couldn't live forever, so he went on to become immortal.

Don't ever let your body hear you speak of getting old.

We All Have the Seeds of Death or Immortality Within Us

You come into this life with the seed of death. A death program is even in the DNA. There is a genetic and spiritual seed which is coded for death that we too often want to embrace. If you don't embrace life, the seed of death (which we are pregnant with from birth as it has been passed down from our ancestors) will dominate.

There is also a drive for life within the body. The question is, how long should we live — eighty-five, one hundred, or one thousand years? Or could it be longer than that? According to legend, one characteristic of the ancient masters was the longevity they manifested. Everyone will form their own attitudes toward aging. Do not believe all you've been taught to believe about getting older. Always listen to your words and to your thoughts that are not spoken. Don't ever let your body hear you speak of getting old. Just consider the legendary accounts of the biblical multi-centenarians like Methuselah and others. Perhaps the possibility exists. We can choose to do things that enhance our longevity. Do what you can for your own health rather than ask someone to do something for you. Visualize a long life by always seeing yourself as young.

How can we water the seed of physical immortality? One way is to keep growing. Keep evolving. This growth process allows the body to rejuvenate and live purposefully. Keep expanding and learning new things. That keeps us bright and youthful.

Perhaps we could live healthily into our hundreds if we kept ourselves cleansed, ate properly and kept a calm and tranquil mind.

Embrace the Unlimited Life Span

You embrace life by embracing your purpose for being here. Loving life is so important. You need that burning passion of loving life. Everything exists in that love; without it the fire goes out. Most of us have a strong urge to live, and some may even wonder why it's often so hard to die. It's hard to destroy the body. It takes a lot of negativity and abuse. The body can take severe abuse and still make it. Look at people in nursing homes who aren't even aware, or who are in terrible pain, and yet choose to continue to survive. If we would just focus on life unlimited, how much more life would we add to our days?

You must remain useful. Approach life as if it is impossible to fail; that is the essence of a glorious life. Every area of life lived with mastery is a life well lived. To live this life of mastery calls for vigilance and discipline. Time will pass whether you use it purposefully or not.

At bedtime, think back on the day in reverse. Lie in bed and recreate it as a meditation where you think back moment by moment through the entire day. This will help you weave the threads of eternity together. This daily process will begin to thread the gems of wisdom together and create a stream of consciousness. After this you can thread not only the day but a week, a month, years, to birth and for lifetimes. This process will eventually reveal your own immortality. You will begin to realize that you've always been alive in one form or another, and you get a hint that you can remain alive, in this form, for as long as you choose if you're conscious and careful.

Staying Alive Is an Art Form

In order to enjoy the happenings on earth, you have to stay alive. The number-one killer is heart attacks. Number two is cancer, and third is strokes. Number four is influenza, and the fifth, accidents. This fifth-largest killer, accidents, is the most challenging because it calls for awareness. Awareness to avoid accidents calls for being conscious in the moment. If you're really conscious, you'll never get sick at all, or get hit by a truck.

**Life Is Luminous When You
Have the Courage To Live It**

Growing old is not for wimps. Age does not matter as long as you are young at heart. It is the zest for life that makes for youth. In the Georgian region of what was formerly known as the USSR (prior to the difficulties in the '90s where violence led to early death), people lived very active lives well into their hundreds and beyond. The same is true of Vilcabamba, Ecuador, other spots in the high Andes, and Hunza in the high Himalayas. It might be noted that the average caloric intake was 1,600 calories per day for Vilcabamba and 1,800 calories per day for Hunza.

So many beliefs about aging are not real but become so when we embrace them and act them out on this stage of life. The old teachings are collapsing. Continue to question old belief patterns that may need to go by the wayside.

Studies have shown that our bodies will reproduce themselves only so many times before they die. According to one researcher, the cells of our bodies double approximately 50 times and no more. That is called the Hayflick limit. However, vitamin E intake, such as is found in wheat germ, will allow the cells to double up to 120 times. So if the average life span is 70 years, with the proper vitamin E supplementation, longevity should greatly increase. Is it feasible that a person might live twice the average age?

> *The person who is focused*
> *and loves life stays alive.*

To Stay Alive, Stay Productive

People have to take certain measures to stay alive. A primary measure is to remain productive. This does not mean having offspring! Being productive is to demonstrate productivity, and it is productivity that keeps us alive.

After the sexual functioning begins to slow down and stops, most people live another twenty to thirty years. But with goals and purpose, you stay alive even after the sexuality atrophies.

At the onset of late fall and prior to winter, drone bees are hauled out of their hives by the wings and dropped over the side. The worker bees who are productive are the ones that get to stay around because there is only so much food, and nature dictates that the useless will not be fed.

Are you working and productive in some capacity? This productivity and work does not necessarily mean being tied to a job. What is it you are doing that is creative and productive? Consider how you can improve your creativity and productivity.

The common threads of longevity include:

1. First and foremost, a rationally healthy mind
2. Clean air
3. Pure water
4. A low-fat, low-calorie diet
5. Exercise
6. A favorable climate
7. Productive, purposeful and creative work
8. A strong love for life
9. Not dwelling on "what ifs" or life-threatening issues
10. Daily inspirational readings
11. Listening to or playing healthy, wholesome music
12. Positive accomplishments and a sense of fulfillment

Visualize a long life by always seeing yourself as young.

QUESTIONS AND ANSWERS

Would you tell us about your dietary habits? I know they have to do with your thoughts on how diet affects longevity and immortality.

I'll give you the dehydrated, freeze-dried answer, John. To begin with, I don't eat anything with a face. Other than that, I eat like a primate with one exception — the amount. It takes very little to maintain my 200-pound body.

I eat one major meal per day, which is a fresh and raw salad with extra-virgin olive oil and apple cider vinegar with the "mother" in it as a dressing. I enjoy an occasional glass of dry, red wine, soft music, incense made from a wood with a special time-honored fragrance and several uninterrupted hours to consume this nourishment at midafternoon. I drink plenty of distilled water.

Generally, Ann and I have up to a quart of carrot juice in the morning, or we have Dr. Richard Schulze's super food drink blended with strawberries, bananas and fresh, organic apple juice. Other than a little snacking and our nightly "Merrwe Wabbit," which is described elsewhere in this book, my herbal "kundalini accelerator extract" and a few herbal supplements, that's it!

In the minds of most, that diet should create an undernourished frail shadow of a human. They are not unjustified in their viewpoint. Many vegetarians are emaciated, skinny weaklings that must fear even an autumn breeze. Contrast that with a gorilla or even a chimpanzee. The chimp has more than eight times the strength of an adult male human. I have even seen a gorilla in a zoo stretch a truck tire like a rubber band — and he did this on his natural, fresh and raw diet.

It is telling when we see our chemically enhanced athletes, bodybuilders and power lifters, many of whom appear to die at such young ages, not able to compete against the strength of some of our great apes who are basically fruitarian.

On occasion, some very strong men will visit me, having heard stories about my strength. On these occasions I might take out a steel spike, a piece of iron rebar or a horseshoe and allow them to attempt to bend it. You can likely guess the outcome. Then, when I do bend whichever of these three objects, they look at me as if it is a trick. Well, what can you say? When I take a sledgehammer and hold it straight out, horizontally, by the tip of the handle, they can't understand where the strength comes from. Of course, there is no denying that exercise plays a part. But it is inconceivable when performed by an "old man" who abandoned the steak and potatoes meal set many decades ago. Why can't they compete? Perhaps they should ask a gorilla.

Strength, health and vitality do not result from food as much as from the vibration or energy present within the food. In a healthy adult, the same amount of food that goes in must come out in order for health to exist. It is shameful to pack our skin bag with pounds of rotten feces and carry it around with us for years. Some autopsies have shown many people to have had as much or more than fifty pounds of hardened feces, stones and other debris locked up in their colon.

The length of the alimentary canal in humans and primates is very long, being twelve times the length of the body. In carnivorous animals the alimentary canal is only three times the length of the body. The entrance-to-exit time is very short. That allows the carnivore to quickly process its meal so it will not be poisoned by the toxins of the meat.

When the venous blood that brings waste products out of the body via the eliminating organs is stopped by the death of the animal, the arteries continue to contract forcing the remaining blood to saturate the tissues. Thus, it is impossible to extract these poisons from the body, especially at death.

If you could take a piece of meat and wash out of it all the poisonous juices that are usually expelled by the elimination organs, you would end up with something akin to tasteless plastic. You see, it is the excrement that gives meat its flavor. This also gives rise to the high uric acid found in the urine of meat eaters. This strong odor is the result of all the cell nuclei decaying in the meat.

In vegetarian animals the reaction is mostly alkaline if no meat has been eaten. It is interesting to note that dogs and cats can be quite free of uric acid due to the difference in their physiology. In a human, the uric acid passes through the liver where it is turned into urea which damages and robs strength from the human body.

We must rely on our saliva to break down our food, as does the ape. The carnivore has but very small salivary glands. He has a round, expansive and very simple stomach and food does not stay there long. Ours and the ape's stomachs are complex: They have a mucous membrane covered with many valvular folds. Meat-eating animals have a rough tongue that they use for lapping fluid, whereas we and the other primates have a smooth tongue and drink by suction. In fact, have you ever wondered why a dog will not eat a cat but a cat will eat a mouse? Why is it that carnivores are not eaten? Why is it that a carnivore will find it safe only to eat a vegetarian animal?

So you see, John, my diet is more in harmony with what nature dictates. And if we are more in harmony, then can we not expect to be better in both health and strength?

Now we must ask what is it in certain foods

that gives such vitality and how does it do that? If the same amount of food that goes into the body comes out, what nourishes the physical form? John, you've seen all the bears we have. Now, just consider Chaser for a moment. He is around 500 pounds. His fur just glistens from the sunflower seeds he consumes. How does all this take place when the very same seeds that go in, come back out — many in the same whole form that entered his mouth? What contributes to his size?

It is just like a tree growing in a large clay pot. If you weigh the soil when the tree is a foot tall and then again when it is ten feet tall, the soil will weigh the same. Trees don't eat soil. The soil only provides a magnetic anchor, and like a battery, water is needed to help provide a charge. Just like the cells of our bodies, they have both a negative and positive pole. Cells are batteries that hold our pulse of life. When the charge is low, so is our energy. When the cell can no longer hold its charge, it dies, just like what happens to our cars if we leave the lights on without the motor running.

I could go into greater detail about the

entire process of cell degeneration, but the point I want to make is: It is not nutrition, but cell stimulation that results in our physical existence and determines the state of our health.

Consider how a sprout, a leaf, or a flower grows by the stimulation of sunlight. The light creates the green blood of plants called chlorophyll. The chlorophyll molecule is almost identical to the hemoglobin molecule that carries oxygen via the red corpuscles of our blood to charge our bodies with life force. The only difference between them is that the central atom in chlorophyll is magnesium, which allows for the greenness of a leaf, versus the central atom of iron in hemoglobin, that allows our blood to be red. So it is an interesting fact that when we consume chlorophyll we enrich our blood and its ability to utilize oxygen. The central atom in chlorophyll transmutates in our bodies from magnesium into iron — an amazing fact in itself!

It is said that the quality of our blood determines the quality of our body, which is the result of the quality of our food. So what are the cells made from? They are made from molecules. What are molecules made of? Atoms. What are atoms made of? Electrons, protons and other subatomic particles, which are in fact not particles at all but pure vibration. Wave fonts of certain frequencies are what both food and the body are made of.

Do these subatomic, wave-font particles eat? No. They do not eat any more than a star eats the sky or a tree eats the soil. Since these subatomic wave-font particles do not eat and construct what we call an atom, and atoms make up molecules which construct cells, how can cells eat? They do not eat, nor do they grow by the food they consume. It is vibration and vibration alone that stimulates cell growth and multiplication. The tremendous vibration found in live, uncooked fruits, vegetables and herbs that stimulate the cell in the same manner that a magnet spinning around a copper coil produces electricity. How very simple, yet extremely mysterious.

It is said we are a race of overfed and undernourished people. To be more precise, there are just a lot of folks with bad vibration and clogged colons. People race so fast that they never seem to get the time to evacuate their bowels. It is important to note that the healthier you are, the shorter the time between mouth and toilet. The sicker and more decrepit, the longer the time between meal and defecation. If you eat three times a day, although eating that much is ridiculous, you must have three bowel movements per day! Never eat another meal until you have eliminated the previous one. That's the royal road to luminous health; yet, most of our population, the medical profession included, consider one bowel movement every three days normal. I say you're abnormal if you don't have three per day if you're eating that many meals.

Again, we appear to be a world of people where everyone wants to hang on to their sh—! After all, what do people talk about? Just listen and you'll hear a litany of woes. They just can't seem to drop the past. Until they do, no amount of laxatives will move their bowels or establish health. Health is as much mental as it is physical.

Abundant health is only possible where there is abundant love in one's life. And if you want to be loved, you must first be lovable. You must first find out who you are. When you do, when you fall in love with yourself for the very first time, you have fallen in love with God. Now your needs have fallen from you. Your hands are empty.

Now you can embrace eternity and now true health has returned. You now know about longevity and immortality because you are approaching it.

Follow this path, and good health to you!

In seminars you have said, "We are the tree of life. We were designed for eternal physical life on earth." Why have we not seen this?

We have not seen eternal physical life because we have become a defoliated race, barren branches devoid of fruit, flower and fragrance, offering no one shelter. Distrustful and cynical, we have broken our own bones and every little bug and creeping thing has gotten under our bark and eaten out our hearts. We, who destiny has beckoned forth to embrace eternity, settle for a paltry three score and ten. Shame. Yes, may shame fill us at our beggarly choice.

Our bodies are forever young, our hearts are the fountains of youth and our blood the river of life. Old age is a myth. Our bodies are never more than one to seven years old at any given time. Then why do we look so bad? Why do we suffer from the afflictions we call disease? There is no aging. The revolving of the earth around the sun has no effect whatsoever on our cells any more than the moon wears out because of its orbit around the earth. There is no aging! There is no such thing as disease! There is only decrepitude.

No machine repairs itself. It requires nuts to be tightened, springs, pistons and parts to be replaced. It is powerless to do this itself. Consider if the machine were able to continually repair itself, making it incapable of wearing out, it would last forever. Man has erroneously been compared to a machine; and yet, unlike the machine, the human body is constantly repairing itself even when we have sewage sludge pumping through our veins and blood pudding for brains. The healing process remains and cuts heal in the same manner whether we are nine or ninety. The fact remains undisput-

ed: The physical body is self-generating, self-renewing, self-sustaining, self-governing and self-adjusting. No machine can do that; if it could, the machine would be immortal. The body dies only because it has been suffocated in its own filth and can no longer adapt to its poisonous and hostile environment.

When cells are no longer able to illuminate with the spark of life, they begin to decay and contaminate the fluid they swim in, which is what decomposes the cell. The gases of our decomposed cells then pass with each exhalation, poisoning a fifty-five gallon drum of normal air, making it unfit to breathe. We then stupidly breathe the expelled poisons contained in the little cells we work and live in and drowsily go about the business called life, charged up or sedated depending on the time of day, with our newest designer drug.

It is sad that we still labor under the misconception that it is what we put into the body that results in health instead of realizing it is just the opposite — it is what we get out of the body that results in health. So if you ignore this fact and continue to ingest your Halcion,

Tagamet, Prozac and Reglan for your temporary peace of mind, please avoid reading the side effects listed on the container. The side effects produce everything from symptoms of Parkinson's disease to amnesia, and liver dysfunction to cancer. Also ignore the fact that each year 1.6 million people end up in hospitals because of these effects, not to speak of the 160,000 who never get out! They die. That's 160,000 people each year!

I am certain you have heard about the drug Viagra for curing impotency. Talk about side effects! The news media reported shortly after the drug was made available to the public that seven men had died when they mixed it with the favorite choice of heart medication, nitroglycerin. I find it amusing that we now need a drug to keep us pumping around like rabbits in a hutch. A renowned endocrinologist reported he had never seen a eunuch live over sixty years. And no one sees a correlation between that and a society of people who with regularity deplete their hormonal reserves? And yet they wonder why they continue to become increasingly obese, with graying and balding heads and wrinkled flesh? Why accept premature and accelerated aging while perpetual youth is still an option?

The body does not wear out like a machine and passing time does not age it. With each passing day and each new bout of ill health and ingested poisons, vitality decreases. We overburden ourselves by unnatural living. And when the burden becomes more than we can carry and adapt to, we die. Consider the function of a sump pump being used to pump out rising flood waters from a person's home. The pump keeps working perfectly, but unable to handle the volume of incoming seepage, becomes submerged and ceases to function. There was nothing wrong with the pump — it just couldn't operate underwater.

As an example, having breast examinations for that deadly cancerous lump appears prudent, yet by the time you find that lump the cancer is anything but a new discovery in your body. In fact, researchers state that there are at least an average of 45 billion cancer cells already multiplying in the body. This year there will be 180,000 women diagnosed with breast cancer.

Even though the herb curcumin (turmeric)

has been shown to inhibit cancer cell growth and has a powerful effect on estrogenic activity, health results from what we pump out of our bodies, not what we pump into them. The design and function of our immune system is perfect; it is just overwhelmed by the toxic substances that flood the body.

A similar situation is found with men. The prostate gland, like all the other glands and organs in the human body, operates with perfection until, like our water pump, it is overwhelmed. And then the medical professionals tell us the gland wore out and couldn't handle the conversion of testosterone into dihydrotestosterone. We didn't wear them out; we overwhelmed them.

The human body, unlike a machine that is unable to repair itself, is always self-renewing and will be until the flood of external pollutants overwhelm it and force it to shut down. The cause of death is always suffocating oneself in one's own ingested waste or overwhelming the system externally with a polluted and toxic environment. That is what the experts label disease, and they give them all sorts of medical names.

Fifteen years ago I wrote a booklet (out of print at present) called, How Long Do You Choose To Live? — The Ultimate Healing Decision. *In it I addressed the issue of physical immortality. By that I mean, unlimited physical life span — perpetual youth. Fifteen years ago the idea appeared absurd to most people. Now, with greatly enhanced scientific research and understanding available to us, extended life spans into our hundreds are no longer mythical. Yet, ancient sages and obscure texts assert that physical immortality is not a myth but a living reality, and an option for those who are courageous enough to pursue it.*

When a car is rolling downhill, isn't applying the brakes the first thing you do? Likewise with the issue of aging. Since our inherited genetic momentum is powerful and our load of accumulated waste large, it takes a number of years to stop it. Then a point of equilibrium is reached. That's when the processes of decay and repair are equal. What is termed old age is when decay outweighs repair. And youth is when growth overcomes decay. In the balanced state of anabolism and catabolism, the state where waste does not overwhelm repair, the body remains in a state of non-aging. And if the state is continuously maintained, the result is physical immortality. After stopping the roll downwards, you can make your goal to be a year younger as each calendar year rolls forward. Barring accidents and "the bomb," you can live forever.

You are the tree of eternal life in the garden of God consciousness.

This chapter mentions one of the leading causes of death, AIDS. Do you have any insights you would like to share?

As it has been reported, AIDS appears to be directly linked to unsafe sexual contacts, contaminated blood and the sharing of unsterilized needles. I also find it of interest that in Third-World countries, AIDS is rampant throughout all sectors of society. AIDS showed up in full force in Haiti after the World Health Organization administered hepatitis B vaccine. In the Dominican Republic, the half of the island that did not get the vaccine had relatively few cases. This same story is repeated in Africa. Since this is just an observation, people will have to draw their own conclusions.

How is hepatitis B spread? It is spread through sexual contact, contaminated blood and the sharing of unsterilized needles. Who gives blood today? Who needs money the most? Yes, many donors, particularly in cities, are those who need the money, many of whom are street people, alcoholics, drug addicts and prostitutes. I have heard that the hepatitis B vaccine is made from the blood of these donors.

People infected with hepatitis B, a precursor of AIDS, experience dark urine, flu-like feelings, extreme loss of appetite, joint pain, fever, hives and so on. It also attacks the liver, giving one a jaundiced appearance in the advanced stages. Infected people just don't have any energy.

One of the most interesting aspects to me is that interferon therapy is an FDA-approved alternative to combat this disease. One effect of interferon in our blood is that it strengthens the immune system. It also causes changes in personality, seen in individuals becoming more force-

ful and decisive. Studies have shown that the more forceful and decisive we become, the more effectively the thymus gland operates. Under acute distress, the thymus gland, which is the key gland of the immune system, can shrink to one-half its size in a twenty-four-hour period. In an experiment with rats, when the thymus gland was impaired the rats became overly sexual, requiring many partners followed by sudden onset of malaise, loss of appetite, fever, hives and dark urine. The mice became very thin and decrepit and then died.

Consider that by changing your attitude toward life, by taking more personal responsibility, becoming more decisive, and thinking more rationally and clearly, you could greatly enhance your immune system. The good news is, you can if the "I Will" is present.

The chemicals of mental attitudes have been identified as neuropeptides. More than fifty-six different neuropeptides have been studied, many of which were found to be hormones which we used to believe were only produced by the glands, not the nerve cells. It is now known that your emotions affect the production of T cells and B cells and that one of the chemicals secreted by them is interferon!

Neuroscience, endocrinology and immunology are loudly sending us signals: Change your attitude if want to live. If a person changes his attitude, he will automatically change his behavior and thus the circumstances of his life as well. I firmly believe, as a man thinketh in his heart, the seat of emotion, so he is!

Wealth

Creating Wealth

Creating Wealth Can Be Magical

We don't have to search for wealth on the outside. It comes first from the inside and then manifests outwardly. Remember, it's not what we want but what we are that comes to us. Anyone can spend a lifetime collecting money and becoming a millionaire, but being a millionaire is rather ordinary. At times being a millionaire doesn't even make one prosperous, because if the millionaire is always wanting more, he'll always be impoverished.

Having money is not what makes one wealthy. The difference between a wealthy man and an impoverished one is that the wealthy individual feels complete with or without money. It is not having more or having less that makes us wealthy.

Once we realize this, we are free for the "magnet" of wealth to create prosperity in our lives.

The magic lies in the "Monte Carlo effect." This is a gambling term which says that you can roll sixes every time, or "box cars" or whatever it is, because every single time you act, each roll of the dice is independent of the others. When we put independent events together and come up with the same results each and every time, we call it magic. There is no reason not to come up with sixes every time because each roll of our life is independent of the one before. Winning is not a sometimes thing, it is an all-times thing.

Make Wealth A Preference, Not a Demand

The thing that keeps us from being affluent is that it is so obvious how wealth is created that we don't see the means. When we begin to demand wealth, it becomes an addiction in terms of "have tos" and the addiction blocks the flow. We make it a struggle, whereas wealth is magical and magic is a common aspect of everyday life.

Life is all cause and effect. If you don't like what you are getting, change the cause. The cause is always "stinking thinking," consciously or unconsciously. Our attitude is the expression of our expectation of results from the world around us. When you change your attitude you change the results, but you can only change your attitude by changing your expectations. The secret of prosperity is knowing that you get what you set.

If your programmed expectations are that you must earn your bread by the sweat of your brow, these expectations then become a curse of survival which leads to suffering, toil and grief. You will for certain resent wealth. You will repel it like countless millions do daily. Your deeply programmed attitude will reveal a cynical and critical expectation — and the result? Poverty and self-sabotage.

Wealth Is Your Birthright

Our magnet is the law of intention, shown as easily as, say, programming yourself to awaken at a certain time in the morning. In fact, how do you wake up two minutes before the alarm clock rings? People will say, "I don't know, except that it was my intention to." It is the same with a wealth magnet: You always find yourself at the right place at the right time. Our essence does not change, but the form does. The original essence goes back to our beginning and the four elements of atomic structure that create the force field of attraction and the power of an indwelling intention. When we experience glimpses of the essence of our being, we begin to understand that magnet. There is a force of intention that allows us to attract and manifest all the things we call wealth, such as happiness, health, financial security, comfort, relationships and spirituality. Consider this as your high ideal, to understand what you really want and to follow your soul's expression and its intention to manifest.

There may come a time when you look at wealth in terms of emotional happiness or an artistic or poetic expression. At these times you must relax and undo certain things so that your original form, your original essence, can return. In the total universal scheme there is nothing wrong with any of us. It is a matter of relaxing and unknotting our lives.

All of our teachings are borrowed until we experience, examine and test them for ourselves. Recognize what you haven't personally experienced for yourself and learn from others who have discovered the source of the wealth magnet. Find others who are living examples of the substance that goes far beyond the norm.

We are the pure essence. In our "higher atmosphere" we are pure, untainted and unpolluted. However, like the rains from the heavens, falling through the atmosphere to the soil, we take on certain qualities as we go along. Once we were fine, but we've gotten a little tarnished along the way. We have to be refined by finding that essence again. The closer we get to refining ourselves (re-finding that essence), the richer we become. As we become rich in substance, we hand life a bouquet — and it hands it right back. Your wealth is your birthright. If you want it, you can have it. When you find your inner richness, it becomes effortless.

Recognize Your Richness

We must recognize our richness inside or we will feel victimized. Parado's Law of economics found that approximately eighty percent of the population does nothing while the remaining twenty percent supports the eighty in some way. Economists have now discovered that only three percent of the population is creating the wealth for ninety-seven percent of our society. In other words, if you took one hundred people, three out of the hundred would be conscientious and applying themselves.

We recognize that there are many who are slothful. Too many in our country hold to concepts that do not allow for the reward of the individual. Since 1960 in the United States, there has been an increase in the propagation of a socialist agenda which encourages belief in a free lunch, a "do it for me" mentality.

The happiest and most successful people are those who have taken control of their own lives and understand that freedom comes only with responsibility. While we live in a free enterprise system, most fail to realize that the more enterprising they are, the freer they become. If we're not in control, we feel we are victims; and when we feel victimized we get vindictive; and when vindictive, we are volunteers for our own economic and emotional demise.

There is great opportunity today for increasing wealth and health and happiness. The opportunities are always before us, but we must mine our opportunities. We mine them by the application of conscious energy toward our high ideals. We then allow the powerful magnet of our deep-seated intention to draw the appropriate results into our lives.

Learn to Create Wealth Effortlessly

The key to being an alchemist with wealth is making it a game and not a "have to". A lighthearted attitude allows us to create wealth effortlessly. It is difficult to be around serious, somber people where everything is an issue. When we become serious, we attach an obsession to things and cling and rush and bring addiction into the picture. Tension is created when we lose the playful attitude. We have to remember that there have been times when we lost money, times when we failed, times we missed hitting the ball in the game of life, but it wasn't the end of the world.

This life is nothing but opportunity. Create a vacuum and something always comes in. It happens quickly, faster than you might imagine. You've been around before. Relax, lighten up.

If you know why you're here and what you're to do in this life, the "stuff" that happens doesn't bother you as much. Don't worry about it. Allow your life to be effortless and your intentional energy will flow to wealth in any form you desire. Life is just that magical. Life is so easy when it is a game, but the moment you take it seriously you suffer.

Material richness is gained when you know that if you lose you can still play again. If you start taking the game of life too seriously, it is going to be too stressful and then mistakes are likely.

The Kingdom of Heaven is inside you, and the gates to heaven open wide with sincerity, not seriousness. When the playfulness is gone, you can't win. If you burn out, spend time by yourself, go to the country, be in silence and rejuvenate. Relax, take the knots out of life. Learn to create wealth effortlessly with the tools of intention and the clear vision of your high ideal.

Money Is a Product of Your Creativity

Money is a measure of production. You earn money by being productive, and productivity is born of your creativity. Envious people want the unearned. Seek the earned by being productive and then you help the world by not being a burden to others. Being self-sufficient is very refreshing.

The Tenfold Return

By being generous you create wealth and prosperity. There is a universal law called the tenfold return. Every generosity can be considered a seed planted, with a harvest promised of a tenfold bounty. These are ordinary laws of the universe that make for an abundant reality.

Mental fortitude and tenacity are attributes that give birth to wealth. Since there is not enough time to work on everybody else, work on yourself so the world will never be called on to take care of you.

Energy Is Wealth, Wealth Is Energy

If you really want money to work for you, do not limit it with impoverished thoughts. You cannot believe that money is evil and then expect to manifest prosperity! Do not hold onto an old conditioning of scarcity. This belief is subtly impressed on tender minds when a mother doesn't have enough breast milk to offer or when parents fight at the dinner table over the budget. It may be as simple as always finding an empty refrigerator. It is a particularly insidious teaching when it comes in the form of "because they have it all, we don't have enough." Paradoxically, the feeling of scarcity leads to the tendency to hoard. Hoarding will actually cost you money. Hoarding does not allow for the free flow of money, for hoarding does not allow money to multiply and prosper. Money must be used and properly invested in order to multiply. Since all investments carry a degree of risk, a person steeped in scarcity is emotionally unable to deal with the threat of loss and thus is bound to remain impoverished.

When I asked Peter about hoarding, this is what he replied: "Consider a man who will not add an additional page to a letter because it will cost extra postage and yet week after week plays the lottery in hope of becoming a millionaire. This person has scarcity consciousness so deeply ingrained in his psyche that no matter what opportunities come his way, his old programming will sabotage him. It reveals a stinginess on one hand and a something-for-nothing mentality on the other. Where did it come from?

"It can be explained as simply as a parent saying to a child who put a quarter in his mouth, "Spit that out, it's dirty!" How few of us see the connection between "dirty" money and "Blessed are the poor." Who of us can sanely state that poverty is a blessing? It is only the case when there is a limiting of addictions and desires, but that is rarely the case.

"The stingy man continues to grope for the approval to be blessed and to get to live in a mansion in heaven and walk on streets paved with gold; yet, in this life he was so stingy that he never had a dime to share with anyone. He stands more of a chance of winning the jackpot or a sweepstakes. If that's his mentality, in my mind he's a crackpot."

Create the Feeling of Wealth

Cash can be carried to give the feeling of wealth. Do not be afraid to carry a hundred-dollar bill or several hundred-dollar bills. It is not the same as plastic that you must pay for later. Having money in your pocket is granting yourself permission to purchase what you want, when you want, and never have a debt. Consider window-shopping without money; it doesn't feel good. But consider the paradox: When you have money, you don't feel compelled to spend it frivolously. Carrying several one hundred-dollar bills has a powerful psychological effect.

Universal Laws

Help people get what they want in life, and you'll always get what you want. Help others and they will help you; that's a part of the universal law. Another part of the universal law is that wealth in this nation will ultimately be in the hands and holdings of those who deserve it. Don't be despondent or discouraged when the cycles occur. Discouragement leads to disheartenment which means that we have given up love and brightness.

Manifesting Prosperity

You will only have money if you have something to do with it. If you do not know what you want to do with money, there is no place for it to go and it will not be created. Not only do you have to figure out how you would earn it, you must figure out what you would do with it.

To experience the joy of giving abundance away, you have to have it first. You must have goals and apply energy to the fulfillment of those aspirations — even if they seem to be a little beyond your reach — or you will not live fully. Give your brain a detailed and clear message to work on something.

A sense of achievement cubes itself. The further along you have come, the easier it is. This is true with health and also with wealth. A millionaire finds it easy accumulating $100,000 because his or her mind is trained to work that way. It is much more difficult for a poor person to save a hundred dollars.

Money is your permission slip.

The Moth Comes to the Flame

Set Financial Goals

Make your financial goals reachable by stretching for them. A goal is not a goal if you can already reach it. If you put down on paper that you will increase your income by 25 percent, this may not be reachable by working for the same person you are now. Break it down into twelve months and you'll do extraordinarily well. What gets measured gets done. Know what you need to make as each month's goal. Then increase your service and its quality and you'll be noticed. Maybe you will not be noticed by your current employer, but even so, you may end up being offered a new position by someone else who sees your excellence.

Start out by saving from your paycheck a minimum of l0 percent. Pay yourself first and put this money aside for investment. Plant it, forget it and let it grow. This will make you feel somewhat more whole and secure. The next year save l5 percent and keep increasing it until you reach the 25 percent.

Learn to invest. Investing creates interest. You must invest in something that yields interest or you will create very little. Keep in mind the hourglass and how quickly those little grains of sand accumulate.

Build on solid foundations, don't "fake it until you make it." When you build on substance, you can build as high as you like. Then the magic takes hold. It takes practice. You will create results in your reality in equal measure to either your inspiration or your fear. Be motivated by inspiration.

The More Self-sufficient You Are, the Fewer Problems You'll Have

A few years ago, very wealthy U.S. citizens made up 1/2 of 1 percent of the population. On average, they hold 2.5 million dollars of worth each. The other 1/2 of the top 1 percent is comprised of about 420,000 people. Each of these 420,000 people, on average, holds 1.7 million dollars in wealth.

The next 9 percent of the U.S. population are considered rich. On average, they hold $419,000 net worth. The remaining 90 percent, on average, are worth $40,000. That includes house, car and everything else. That's averaged. Many in this 90-

percent class have nothing. The top 10 percent have 72 percent of all private holdings. But remember, most worked very hard for their wealth, though some are beneficiaries of trust funds and inheritances. What would happen if the top 10 percent quit working and did not earn money? What would happen to the other 90 percent who are dependent upon them for employment and livelihood? The top 10 percent, who own 72 percent of all holdings, actually keep the country going.

Educate yourself so you can be more independent and self-sufficient. How can you help the welfare system? Don't be on welfare. Don't be dependent upon any social system. That life raft is so crowded it's about to sink, and that's not to even speak of the hole in its bottom.

According to the U.S. Department of Labor, 97 people out of 100 will, by age 65, have to depend on a social security check to live. Do what it takes to responsibly become independent. Don't be one of the above 97 out of 100.

Money Is Energy

Money is permission as well as a unit of production. Earning money is an expression of your creativity. Fully realized people have both time and money. They know what the requirements for living are. There is no virtue in always struggling just to exist. They can live simply and be full of real abundance. Actually, simple living with no addictions or complications is the most prosperous way to enjoy this journey called life.

If you took away all the money from everyone and redistributed it evenly, in a few years it would be right back in the original hands. It would be back in the hands of the people who work and know how to manage and attract money. Money is energy. It will go to where it is energetically created. One of the laws is, "To one who has, more shall be given." This law is based on an attitude of affluence.

Those who have eyes to see and ears to hear experience an abundant and prosperous universe. An abundant attitude does not beg. Beggars will always want more because they live a life of addiction.

You Are Worthy of Having Wealth

Wealth is an everlasting flow of energy. There is always sufficient money to get done what needs to be done. If you want more, empty your cup first and the money will come. As an example, if you want new clothes you must first make room in your closet. Quit believing in scarcity. Quit believing there is not enough stuff to go around. You have to believe it's OK to have good things. You are worthy. If you were unworthy you wouldn't be reading this now.

Wealth is your energy,
and your energy is what creates materiality,
and hidden in the materiality
is divinity and spirituality.

QUESTIONS AND ANSWERS

A friend asks, "Why do humans value that which is earned through struggle more than they value that which is freely given?"

It is an excellent question and an interesting occurrence. First, let us examine the issue of inheritance. This is a charged and tremendously explosive issue. It is tainted with guilt. Consider, from childhood on you have watched your parents slave and save for retirement. They suddenly pass away before they can benefit from a lifetime of hard labor. You feel this is grossly unjust. You feel life has cheated them. In other words, the laws of reaping and sowing, cause and effect, appear out of order. And now you, who have done nothing, are in line to receive an unexpected bounty. You are filled with a deep-seated sense of unworthiness and guilt. How can you profit from a loved one's demise?

This destructive, psychological undercurrent keeps many people bound in poverty. The mind irrationally concludes that if they remained in need, then upon the death of their parents they would feel more deserving. After all, who could now blame them? They are struggling, poor and desperate. How would it look if they were rich and now receiving? And after all, the Bible states that we are doomed to earn our bread by the sweat of our brow. And now you are enjoying a bountiful inheritance? Heaven forbid! And we wonder why so many who win lotteries seem to have the money vanish as if it were cotton candy?

Now let us examine struggle. Struggle is always mental. Take two men digging in a garden. One man owns the land and the other is hired for the day. To the one, the digging holds promise, to the other just the passing of time. To the one it is struggle; to the other it is hope. Someone put it beautifully this way, "Work is what you do when you would rather be doing something else." In that context, struggle is just a bunch of work.

Struggle implies the expenditure of vast amounts of energy. Energy is valuable. Thus, what is earned through this, one feels, should be safeguarded, protected. So it is obvious: Struggle produces more value in the mind of the struggler than something that has been given freely but has a hidden price tag of guilt or obligation attached to it.

There is a better way. When vocation transforms into avocation, when work dissolves into play, struggle and guilt disappear. If you struggle, you will live in resentment, and if you feel forced to give, you will give with attachment. No matter how much is hoarded, fear of loss will remain. On the other hand, if you live in guilt and condemn the misperceived injustice of life, you will castigate and condemn the struggler as a hoarder.

The better way is found only by those who have dropped the beggarly rag of guilt and the miser's coat of struggle. Those who walk the better way realize an inner richness so abundant that they are filled to overflowing. So they give freely and receive freely. Giving and receiving are no more an issue than children at play passing a ball around. Once we have dropped our dark motives and shameful imaginings and become as little children, we dance in this heaven called earth. We sing out praises from our hearts, for God's purpose is freedom and freedom is joy!

The Way to Success

Face Challenges

Challenges will always exist, but it is how you view challenges that counts. If you let life become a battle, you will always be frustrated. Frustration is one way of saying that you are ignorant of the solutions that are always present. Frustration indicates you are not thinking clearly enough to move in the direction of the resolution of challenges.

Challenges can on occasion produce lethargy and convince you not to take action. With total commitment you will be highly successful in the face of the most difficult challenges.

Earning Your Success Brings Fulfillment

It is a blessing when you both experience and recognize that you have control over your life. It doesn't "just happen to you." It must be consciously pursued. Nothing happens by accident; there are laws underlying all events. Money has less value if unearned, and the exhilaration of earned money can bear an unexpected harvest.

Even the paperboy can have a feeling of immense fulfillment, a joyful feeling of the earned. There is either a sense of mastery or a sense of servitude, a sense of life or a sense of death, and we choose one in contrast to the other based on our attitude toward earnings. Earn your income doing what you love and you are, in fact, instantly successful.

Try an Experiment with Excellence

Do an experiment over the next thirty days. Determine to do whatever you do so well and at such levels of excellence that not one thing will be left undone. Your life will change. Probably you will get a raise; and if not, the universe will reward you.

In Earning Money, Apply Personal Excellence

When you have it all, your tastes and desires change. You now live life in simple elegance, and you are content to watch the richness of the sunrises and sunsets. You have learned mastery over your environment. You are now satisfied and fulfilled as you apply your special brand of excellence.

Pride Is a Virtue

Pride has been condemned as a vice, but it is a virtue. Arrogance is cheap; pride must be earned. When you have performed with excellence, pride is earned. Be proud of doing what you do and do it well. Find the things you like to do and excel at them. Pride is the warm glow you receive after a job well done. If someone notices, a simple "thank you" is all the reply needed.

*The sweetest fruit is out on the limb.
Reach for it.*

There Are No Causeless Events

There are no accidents or causeless events in the universe. Even what we used to call chaos has been found to have a rhythm and pattern to it.

Successful people are not "lucky." Their preparation has simply met opportunity, and they have said "yes." Say, "Yes, I am capable." When you say "I can," the whole fabric of your life says "yes." This will allow your life to really change.

Winners Win, and Losers Lose

Why does it appear that winners win and losers lose all the time? Attitude chooses the direction. When you change the attitude, you change results. Winners expect to win and losers expect to lose. The universe simply ensures that we get what we set. All you need do is stop doubting the grand possibilities before you.

Substitute the negative emotions which occur when you feel incapable with the emotions of calm assurance and confidence, and your so-called luck will change. You then see the truth of the lyrics of the old Jerry Reed song "When you're hot, you're hot, and when you're not, you're not." It's all just a state of consciousness.

Attitudes separate number one from number two. Winners and losers are always created based on attitude. A number two is capable but has the attitude of not quite making it. Number one has the attitude of a winner. Effective individuals find solutions to problems, not just once in a while but all the while. They know they can deal with any issue and always win.

When you realize you'll be okay, you suddenly are. Winners learn to heal themselves on all levels of life. You can heal yourself mentally, physically and financially by just changing your attitude. Over time you will develop confidence that you can heal anything. If you've done it once, you know you can do it twice and many times more.

When you hold high values, when your priorities are right, you know what is important to you. Add the "I can, I will and I am" spirit and the results will be there. It is time to dispel the myths of "I can't" that choke one's spirit. Choose only those thoughts that are constructive and supportive toward your goals. When you do this, you will soar and be happier and healthier and more prosperous.

It's fun to play the game of life when you know the rules. The ultimate passion play is the love of playing on the big board called life. It is the exhilaration of winning that releases an inner passion.

Refuse to Rush

Refuse to rush. We may work with intensity and passion. We may work with a sense of urgency, but never rush, never race unconsciously. That behavior is an accident waiting to happen.

Use the "Single Handling Law"

When mail comes in, open it, and either throw it out, file it for future reference, or act on it. If it is a bill, write a check immediately, put the stamp on the envelope, and put it in the outgoing mail. This means mail never leaves your hands without a resolution; generally, it simply comes down to "take care of it or trash it."

Competition

Competition breeds excellence. You get better service and do a better job when competitive energies abound. It is competitive demands that drive the financial markets. Healthy competition makes for better producers and greater opportunities; however, compulsive, negative drives are self-defeating. As in all things, balance is the key word.

Never Compromise on Quality

Quality items are the best. A good thing is never cheap and a cheap thing is never good. You don't save money by getting the cheapest thing. Obtain what you can of quality as you can afford to, then add to it as the years go by. Things of quality last. Faster and cheaper does not translate into quality. Quality is not expensive — it is priceless!

The Time is Right

The time is right when the time is right. With awareness we can become responsible for ourselves.

Let your "yes" mean yes, based on an evaluation of all your observations. Find the workable material within you and talk only victories. When you know yourself, you do not need credentials or promotional material. You are who you are — success personified!

Don't Buy into Doom

If you listen to the prophets of doom, you will be limited. Don't buy into doom. Focus your mind on positive results, and you'll find that anything is possible.

Happiness is found in the taste of victory. The victory is really victory over our thoughts, habits, minds and reality. Victory becomes victory over life's challenges, and it is only possible by focusing on positive results.

Be an example for the world.
Control your mind, body, finances,
relationships, angers, fears, and doubts.
Then you shine brightly and become
a creator in your own right.

QUESTIONS AND ANSWERS

Why do so many people find themselves rushing so much?

Let's examine what's really going on. If you are late for an appointment, are you late because there isn't enough time in the day or are you late because you are unaware of what time of day it is? We all know how time is measured. We all have at least some idea of how much activity can fit into a certain time slot.

I am certain almost everyone in this country has at one time or another been to an "all you can eat" restaurant. There are always those few people who have shoveled a tall mountain of food onto their plates so high that when they get back to their table they have left a trail of food behind. Is it not common human nature to silently chuckle at their foolishness? Who could deny the obvious sight of greedy gluttony before them? Now, is there any difference between someone attempting to shove a massive amount of food down their throat in the shortest amount of time, and a person attempting to jam too much activity into a time slot much too small to contain it? Greed is still greed and so is rushing.

Of course, there are also those who are lazy and unaware. Remember, it takes effort to be aware. Lack of effort is just simple laziness. To be unaware of the appointment time you agreed upon is to be lazy. So, we can conclude, if you are rushing, you are either lazy or greedy and most likely both.

Now, to work with a sense of urgency is totally different. It means you understand the importance of the promised time factor and the task undertaken. Urgency is not panic, though it could be, if the word urgent is considered in its common usage.

Never rush, but work with zeal and enthusiasm and you will be greatly rewarded. Give full attention to each moment and be totally in it, and life will bless you with its bounty.

Peter, it seems that many find themselves rushing in order to meet the expectations of too many people. Perhaps this is to "prove their worth" by seeing that things get accomplished, or at least started. The point is, it takes a certain amount of humility, self-acceptance and/or strong conviction to be aware that focusing on just this or just these few things is sufficient. It is sad to see so many folks spending their time and energy trying to "get it all done" when all we really want is peace.

Decisions Bring Solutions

Be Decisive

Think your decisions through, and make your decisions based on reason, not emotion. Then stick to them, and you will not live a life of turmoil.

Quit saying, "I don't know." Be decisive and find out about what you don't know. If you don't choose, life will choose for you. Don't shipwreck your life by being indecisive. Indecision is also a decision by negation, a decision to do nothing. When under stress and there are decisions to be made, tell yourself, "There are no problems without solutions." Be definitive. Definitiveness allows for a longer and healthier life. Definitiveness of purpose is characterized by the words, "I can."

Don't Drift Around Like a Wandering Generality

Pick a direction, plot your course and go forth. When you decide to take another direction, take it and map it out. Don't just drift around like a wandering generality. If you are not making a statement in the world, you will be unhappy. Happiness is doing what you have chosen to do with definitiveness of purpose. The new can be scary, but you'll never sail new oceans if you're afraid of losing sight of the shore. But once you make a decision and reach out, Pop! — it happens. This has been true of everything, from discovering America to landing on the moon. You will have everything you need once you make a decision. The universe is an entire toy box. Pick a toy and play, or sit there and be miserable. If you're wrong, big deal! Make another decision.

Virtue means to manifest values. *Vir* is the root word for "virile" which defines force — an initiating force. A decision made to do something with a beneficial outcome is spiritual. Power is developed by initiating or acting upon a decision. There is no need for spirit or energy if you're not going to use it. Spirit is energy and energy is spirit. Thus it goes without saying, the more "vir" (or energy) you have, the more spiritual you may be. It allows much to be done.

Drop the "what ifs." So what if you're wrong? And what if you're right and don't act?

Every Decision Contributes to Our Glory or Our Demise

Once you've determined not to look back but to go forward, you will say, "I am winning in this game called life." Take a deep breath, calm yourself, bolster your courage, and you will make more correct decisions than poor ones. Make decisions, and if they need to be corrected, they can be. But do make decisions.

Observe how a successful person makes wise decisions that produce life-affirming results. Observe the wealthy person making life-affirming decisions about their wealth. Don't worry about doing things wrong. Worrying about doing things wrong usually paralyzes action. We all have done many things wrong; it's just built into the nature of living, and we can get over it. Life can be a wonderful adventure. Let mistakes be a simple learning tool to help you grow.

At any given moment you can break an issue down into a more black-and-white option if you do not emotionalize it and just stick to concrete facts. Make sure you are not choosing a life-negating position. That's why putting it down on paper works; you get to see the issue without emotions and in a clear and objective light.

As you apply logic and objectivity to your decision-making processes, you'll note that your choices will always be those which make life better. They are not, however, always the most comfortable decisions available.

As was mentioned in a previous section, but bears repeating here: Peter has a friend who was in a very serious accident. Six doctors pleaded with her for consent to amputate her foot. She called Peter for advice. He said, "Let's reason this out together. If I had an infection on the tip of my index finger, which would be the most difficult to do — cut my finger off and grow a new one, or find a way to clear up the infec-

tion? So you see, cutting off your foot is not an option. Since it no longer remains open for consideration, you have made a decision. Now all you have to do is find a doctor who honors your choice and will work with you. That's far easier than growing a new foot."

At the time of the writing she has returned home and is healing and still has her foot.

Making Intelligent Decisions Is the Most Important Thing in Life

Life, health, comfort and peace are all very valuable. Decisions must be made to insure that these things remain safeguarded. Do not identify yourself in light of poor decisions made in the past. The only things we can make choices about are those things before us right now. If you're in a poor marriage, that calls for making a decision today. Either make it better or get out of it because life is simply too important and too short to waste.

Inappropriate employment calls for the same thing. Either make it better or quit. Never wait for a change to occur based on others taking the initiative. Be self-reliant. Learn to cultivate your interest fields. Gain marketable skills. You might want to change your career completely. When the spring starts, the growth starts, and in time the harvest will occur in full measure. Each day is the first day of your life. Today is fresh and new, tomorrow is yet to come, and yesterday is gone. The only decisions you need consider are those which are before you today.

The gold is right where we are. Mine the gold that is before you for all it's worth. Remember, decisions are what get it out of the ground.

Put It on Paper

People who do not make decisions live in hell. Wishes and good intentions never equal constructive positives. It is action, based on clear-cut decisions, that move us from point A to point B to point C. Seize an opportunity immediately when you know specifically what you want. Make the commitment to yourself. This is something that most people never do. Put your plan on paper; always write in the details and facts. What you put on paper must be measurable and quantifiable.

Do not put emotions into the equation as they are fickle and changeable. Once you have set down that which is concrete for your foundation, sign the paper as you would any legal contract for you have just made a binding one for yourself. Putting it on paper is magic.

(Peter says that if it is not on paper, it is not sincere.)

> *You don't have a problem,*
> *only a decision to make.*

Do It Now

Life is about making decisions. Determine what results you want in life and you will know what causes have to take place. What do you want in terms of health, prosperity, peacefulness, joyousness and exuberance and in what definable manner? When people with true internal power work together, they can move cities and the world. When powerful people make decisions, things happen.

*Do all you can, and divine energy
will do the rest; but first,
you must do all you can.*

To illustrate the above point, I quote this short section from a book about Peter written by his friends. The book is titled, The Magic Man.

The way Peter approaches life is a constant inspiration and example of faith and trust. Clearing our property for the building site on Mystic Mountain proved to be a wonderful opportunity for Peter to help us see more clearly the results of total trust in the Divine Plan.

We were cutting to clear the way for electric lines to the Center. The largest of the trees we had cut got caught in the "Y" of another. This always creates a touchy and dangerous situation. We tried our come-along till all the cables were broken. We tried every means at our disposal, but the tree didn't budge an inch. We decided to work further down the hillside.

Hal and Ann were saying that maybe, just maybe, we could get some divine help on this one. It was very hot and we were all a bit edgy — except for Captain Optimism.

Peter sailed down the mountain to start the process again. When we were all out of reach of our hung-up tree — it fell! We couldn't believe it! We had spent two hours trying to do that.

Peter's laughter resounded across the mountainside. We were all suddenly full of energy and happy again, feeling quite in grace. Peter said, "Be aware of this universal truth displayed for you today: Do all you can, and divine energy will always do the rest; but first, you must do all you can."

Another time during the clearing, a large branch with a three-inch diameter broke loose and was falling straight down — perfectly positioned to give Peter a good crack over the head. A few feet above his head, the branch broke in two and fell to either side of him. We questioned him about such good fortune. He said it was "divine insurance" and that it was the best policy he'd ever had.

We were getting the message, and the miraculous examples kept coming and coming.

The Need for Choices

Choosing Tips the Scale of Destiny

Every individual must learn the lesson of choosing wrongly or rightly. There are consequences for acting on poor judgment, and there are blessings that come from proper judgment. A responsible person will ask herself, "What am I going to do about it?"

As we become more responsible, a confidence grows inside us, and we experience a sense of sovereignty — our right to rule responsibly over our own lives.

A World of Pain or Joy

We have a choice to see the world as totally perfect or as totally imperfect. Either the universe and world operate in a perfect, unerring and often unrealized order, or it operates in complete lawless chaos. It cannot operate both ways. Either way we choose to see it, it will appear to be. Everything is working within the framework of cause and effect, so it is perfect in that way. We, in fact, are the only ones who make life a problem.

Any time there is a problem, learn to see that situation as an opportunity to make a decision to change. Of course, you can choose to stay with it and suffer as many do. You can only learn to enjoy challenging times when you are fully conscious. A fully conscious person is aware enough to see all sides of an issue and can choose either pain and anguish, or joy and fulfillment.

Our Freedom of Choice

What do you choose for your life? Perhaps the worst that can happen is to go through this lifetime never making choices, never making decisions, and living simply as a reactionary being. We all have the freedom to make choices; but remember, if we allow that freedom to erode by not using it, only we are to blame.

Life is a game of choice. Read these lyrics of Hal Wilson's song, "Choose Ye This Day":

That which you sow, so shall you reap.
Even as you give, you receive.
Choose ye this day for the light or the darkness.
Choose ye this day who you will serve.

Healthy, wealthy living calls for aware choices. Look deep and make decisions for correct action or you will become paralyzed with inaction. You need not be too analytical about it. Choice also comes with a shadow, and too often it becomes a condition of paralysis by analysis. Indeed, by over-analyzing you get stuck and immobilized in indecision.

It Is Only in This Moment That You Taste Life

Eternity is right here and now. The mind is always in the dead past or the imagined future. It is the mind's function to focus on what was and what is yet to be. The reward of life is in the moment. In the beat of your heart is found the holy drum.

The Moth Comes to the Flame

Listen deeply to the silence between the beats. It is in this space that you taste the divine.

Procrastination is the fear of results. You have the power to choose life second by second; yet, actually it has nothing to do with a clock. You can choose life, love and beauty. There is no time to look at the darkness. It is pointed out only for contrast. Walk toward the light and never look back to see the shadow. It doesn't mean there are no shadows, but they simply do not affect you.

The real question is,
what is it you really want to do?

Work

Make Work Enjoyable

Many people see work as something they do when they'd rather be doing something else. Discover the opportunity to make work enjoyable and playful. See the advantages of being in the workplace. Look at the higher values at stake such as income to insure a family's well-being or to insure happy retirement.

Ask yourself, in the eight hours you work, if you're making the best use of your time. Do you apply yourself and make the best use of your investment of energy?

Choose Wisely

Choose wisely what you would like to do. We do what we want and what we believe we can do. We are only limited by our visions. We are the voice of our own prophecy. Use your awareness and choose your options, or you have chosen to repeat the past. Your habitual patterns will come through unless you consciously choose new directions.

Redefine your responsibilities and do so on paper. How, what, when and with whom questions are essential.

Enjoy productive activity. It is the process — not just the end result — that is so enriching. Many people hate their jobs but do them just to maintain life on earth. There is nothing fulfilling or enriching about that.

Write down a description of what you want. There is no shortage of jobs unless you believe there is a shortage. If the job appears to be non-existent, then create it! It is an excuse to say you are "too old" or that you are incapable of working because of some disability. Oh, yes, there are exceptions; there are those who truly are in need and deserve help, but not the majority. The majority can accomplish almost anything, but first they must choose wisely.

Work Calls for Handling Situations

When work gets tough, handle it. According to Vince Lombardi, famous football coach of the Green Bay Packers, "When the going gets tough, the tough get going." Accept the fact that things don't always run smoothly. See problems not as obstacles, but as stepping stones. Challenges don't get easier, but you can learn to accept them as learning experiences. Act like you're capable of any accomplishment. Find something enjoyable about the work and see it as a game or challenge. Work can become an exhilarating game when we concentrate our energy on the excellence of performance. When we do this, there will be no lack of money or good things in our lives.

Work Is an Expression of Ourselves

The way we express our individuality and our creativity is one of the big keys to our happiness. We have been taught that work is hard, that it is all sweat and drudgery. This is wrong. Work is how we express ourselves.

Explore, don't vegetate. We were created for creative production. No matter what you do, do it with passion, love, creativity and beauty.

**It's Not Doing What You Like,
It's Liking What You Do**

To gain victory over yourself and your employment, you must see yourself as a winner. Approach your workday with a good attitude, anticipating good results. Good attitudes bring good results. Great attitudes bring great results. Fantastic attitudes yield fantastic results. Change the attitude, and you change the results. It works if you work, every single time. So now, plan your work and work your plan.

Love what you do, and you will be successful. Love everything you do and find it exhilarating and successful. Do whatever it is exceedingly well and without complaining. You are never too old for a career you love. Every employer is looking for people who can concentrate on their work — people who are conscientious and can get things done. It is so sad to see laid-off workers in their 40s or 50s saying, "What can I do? I am too old."

It is equally sad to live with the fear of losing a job. Keep up your marketable skills. What can you do that is in demand? Visualize and brainstorm, and then put your ideas on paper and start.

There was a man in Tennessee who was a gas station attendant. He pumped gas and, over time, became the best mechanic they ever had. Eventually he was put on commission. He performed with such excellence he exceeded everyone's expectations in earning power. Eventually he was earning $70,000 a year — and this was in the late 1980s. This is just one of many stories of individuals who planned their work and worked their plans.

Continue to grow, expand, and experience more and more and more. Life will never be the same when you keep reaching.

Work Relationships

If you are unhappy working with another person who is difficult, you can, of course, leave your job; or you can take on more responsibility and thus earn authority. When you gain more control over your work environment, you will be able to beneficially direct others instead of having to deal with them at a level of intimidation.

Remember, even the jerks are part of the reality that you have created. See if you can respond to them in such a manner that they will want to provide service to you.

Take time to ask a person how you can help him. Ask him, "How can I be of better service and make your job easier for you?" What are the facts? Define the job that needs to be done. When, where and by whom? What is expected? Give explanations and allow for questions to be asked. Remember, a job is not a job until everyone knows what is to be done, how it is to be done, and when it is to be done. Make certain neither you nor anyone else is in conflict with the job description. Make absolutely certain that no one is confused about it.

Find workable solutions. There are always alternatives, though not ones you may always want to accept. Let others know your preferences. Ask them what their desires and preferences are. We're not here to change other people or their behavior.

A person who doesn't do his job is a thief. Remember, if someone needs to be fired, it can be done without anger or maliciousness. You can work toward harmonizing a situation by bringing out others' positive work values, but it is thier decision whether or not to improve. If they do not, then they must go. Simply explain that they have violated your work ethics and your conscience, and that unfortunately, their lack of performance does not allow you to fulfill your promises and commitment to the company. One can say, "I have certain responsibilities and commitments that I am obligated to keep. I don't like to do this, but I have to because it is my commitment. I can't go back on it."

To Stay or to Go? Job Conflict

When in conflict, take a piece of paper and fold it in half. On one half write the advantages of staying in a job, and on the other half put down the disadvantages. Whether you stay or go depends on which list is longer. Leave the emotions out of it during this process.

The Moth Comes to the Flame

Be a happy person who freely chooses his work and is fulfilled by it. Learn to love what you do or leave it. We all have many work skills and simply need to choose a destination. Be mindful also that success is not always doing what you like, but more often, liking what you do. The true alchemy is in changing what you don't like into what you do like and making it a game. It's first learning to love what you do and finding ways to make it more creative, exciting and fulfilling. Only then, when you've conquered that situation, are you allowed to go anywhere else.

The universe will repeat those lessons over and over for you until you learn the lessons where you are. People too often go running from one thing to the other, yet universal law says if you still haven't learned a lesson, the teacher will come to you. You cannot run away from the universal divine teacher. He's in every new job you'll get. He's in every new job, every new location and every new relationship.

An evolved and awakened person values work.

Responsibility

Take Care of Yourself So You Won't Have to Be Taken Care of

Become responsible. You will never be free without taking responsibility. Even the person living on the street is not free. The more responsibility we accept, the more freedom and liberation we manifest. Life is magical when we learn the law of cause and effect. You are responsible for you. Be painstakingly honest with yourself. Pick up an issue that needs to be dealt with regarding your life today and take care of it right now.

What are you doing in the present moment that gives birth to freedom and independence? Too many people want to be ruled; it's sad. We abolished slavery, but the slaves wanted to be reinstated. Only the independent person can grant the gift of freedom to others. Balance is the key word. Be self-reliant, cover your bases, and forget about it. Become more responsible for yourself. There are always solutions to the issues of life. Practice what you love. Some of your greatest accomplishments occur when the greatest energy is put forth responsibly. All the years of effort, of applied energy, will move outward and lead to victories. You'll move outwardly to victory, to freedom, to peace.

Victories Are Hollow Without Effort

If an Olympic runner won a gold medal without running for it, it would mean nothing. The gold medal signifies the years of application of intense energy. It is the journey, not the destination, that provides the real fulfillment. Hard work increases the value. People too often want the unearned. The secret of the universe is that "there ain't no free lunch." Live with awareness and reach for the highest that you desire — and be willing to accept responsibility for both success and failure. Follow the rules to the game of life consciously, and you'll find the game works to your benefit. Use your developed tools to create whatever you want. This is being responsible.

"I am lord of my world and the supreme monarch of my kingdom. My crown is my heart, my conscience the royal scepter and reason my book of law. My words are my promise and my promises are my reality. So be it!" - Peter

QUESTIONS AND ANSWERS

I know you are sometimes overwhelmed by people seeking your help. How do you deal with such a burden?

There was a line in a popular song many years ago, "He's not heavy, he's my brother." When Jesus said, "Take my yoke for I am kindly and light," he imparted responsibility to all of us to lighten up and be kind. So few truly understand or differentiate between kindness and weakness. Oh, how my heart aches at the countless times I confused the two! Yes, "He's not heavy, he's my brother..." The Master was once asked how to deal with such situations, how can we carry those who will not walk? How can we see for those who choose blindness? How can we hear for those who have pasted their ears shut? And how can we be kind by being weak ourselves?

Was the Great Teacher cruel by commanding the lame to throw down their crutches and walk? Yes, throw down your limitations, throw down your burdens, throw down your negativity and ego. Throw it down, now! Throw down the weights of a lifetime and then, and only then, can you be embraced by the light for now you are no longer heavy. Now you are my brother, born new in spirit, born anew of a divine mission, born new into a new dawn, the sunrise of your life. But first you must walk, and you will have to walk alone through the valley of the shadow of death.

The heaviness of all the negative habit patterns must be laid down before the test begins. Cruel, maybe. Just? Absolutely! Who is my brother, sister, mother and father? It is only the light illuminating a myriad of worlds as it glistens in a dewdrop. It is the dust of a desert wind and the sting of salty surf upon my face. It is the howl of the wind and the stillness of my heart cave. Yet, is not the seer even greater? For who allows for heavy and light, windy and still? What grandeur is it that sees through the eyes of the seer himself? The Master speaks to me again, "For he who loves mother or father, brother or sister, more than me, is not worthy of me." Yes, brother sun and sister moon, mother earth and divine father, all carry their own loads. Yes, just like the sun, "He's not heavy, he's my brother." Those who are truly your family are never heavy for these are the children of light — and how can you carry those with wings to fly? They are not heavy, they are my brothers.

Overwhelmed... Hmm?... Surprised? Of course not. Suffering is as universal as is seeking relief, and every hand out is a hand down. Anyone can dispense aspirins; only personal responsibility can invoke a cure. Anyone can mouth platitudes; only action can bring relief. The suffering masses appear to be desensitized to suffering. If they really suffered, they would feel compelled to action rather than resignation. Has compassion fled from me because I have found that words don't cook the rice, that nature culls out from before us the weak and sick so that there is room for those who have sought vigor? Are the seasons harsh because the grasshopper is indolent and the ant industrious? Is God cruel to compel the honeybee to throw the lazy drones from the hive at the onset of winter? And is it unfair that our bleeding hearts of weakness have blinded us to kindness? Then I say, seek the counsel of the honeybee and the ant. Should I cry out in anguish because I must work in order to eat? Ask the wolf on a cold arctic night, ask the majestic buck whose herd has been culled. Ask the monarch butterfly why it must flee the cold or why the sandhill crane must fly so many miles. All of the answers are still blowing in the wind.

If we stand still, we die. We all have our seasons and we all have our parts to play. Ask the seer and see through his eyes and the light of justice will shine everywhere. I know my words are not cozy, cuddly and warm. Oh, how my heart aches and my eyes tear. And yet, how can we deny nature and God their sovereignty? So, in the words of Robert Service, "When you're lost in the wild, and you're scared as a child, and death looks you bang in the eye... in hunger and woe, it's easy to blow... it's the hell served for breakfast that's hard."

You bet. Amen. What else can I say? Do you take your coffee black or with cream?

Peter, what about people really in need, like the homeless?

When have we not had the homeless? Consider a state of national emergency — a flood, a fire, a hurricane or a war — and you will find volumes of accounts of people helping people. These events are usually sudden and take people unawares. The polar opposite is the able person who makes one poor decision after another, year after year, never being clever enough to realize or observe the law of cause and effect working in his life. How odd that a person can lose his home and all his belongings and within a short time rebuild and regain his life. A person can flee a war-torn country, leaving everything he spent his life working for, come to a new country with only the shirt on his back and in a few short years become a millionaire.

The Moth Comes to the Flame

As for the bum, he will always remain the same hungry, dependent parasite. Give the bum thousands of dollars and he will only squander and waste it. If you give him a handout, you are now part of his problem, not the solution. Bums are experts at what they do, that is: beg and extort. And don't kid yourself, they laugh behind your back at how they suckered you, then proceed to hunt down another unsuspecting victim. I see them as no different from a vampire who sucks his victim's life blood until they are drained and then looks for another live person to attach himself to. Never give them the time of day, or in this case, night, for they love the darkness.

As I said: They are experts. Yes, they have practiced the sobby tonal inflections and generally have their hard-luck stories honed to perfection. They use their eyes in a persuasive, beseeching manner, often so effectively you may find yourself reaching into your pocket. If you do, consider yourself robbed. No, it wasn't with a gun, it was with tears.

Tears are more powerful than a gun. With a gun you fear losing only your life, but with tears you fear losing your soul. You fear that you are cold, cruel, unloving, uncaring, uncompassionate and that perhaps the punishment for your alleged Scrooge-like behavior is that you will be damned and burn in hell forever. That's a bunch of B.S. Never ever forget — you are the victim and not the other way around! You owe no one an apology for being a self-sufficient, self-reliant, successful, independent person.

Weakness is a crime as well as an extortion. The Latin root word for extortion is torguere *which means to torture by twisting until the victim has been distorted and contorted. When the mutilated body no longer has life, it is thrown into a pit filled with other hapless victims. Whether you are twisted with a rope or tortured psychologically, the extortion is the same. Never forget, it is you who have been victimized, not the other way around! Do not allow yourself to be seduced. They will move into your home and steal everything they can, invite their friends in like a plague of rats and then it will be you who will be forced to leave. I say never crack the door to darkness. If you do, you will regret it as long as you live.*

That's tough talk, Peter.

Unfortunately, not tough enough. My heart aches for so many innocent friends who have been ripped off by these criminals. How can I say it louder without sounding vindictive?

The ABCs of Wealth

The Laws of Prosperity

The laws of prosperity always work. Apply this wisdom and you will see an immediate effect. As we seek to understand these laws, we grow. This takes time, so be patient. If it were time for us to be in the graduate classes, we would be there. Get the ABCs of the material plane out of the way first.

Money used properly and channeled for good does more than speak; it cuts through like a sharp-edged sword. A mentally focused person is powerful with their finances, their physical body, their talents, their virtues, and they are happy in their relationships.

A – ATTITUDE

Our attitude tells the world what we expect, and we always get it. Our attitude is either one of wealth or it is an attitude of impoverishment. Again, our attitude is a direct result of our expectations. Good attitude, good results. Bad attitude, bad results. The law of wealth always works.

B – BEARING

Bearing is how we walk, talk and sit. Observe the way a person's physical form moves and you'll see that 80 to 90 percent of communication is expressed nonverbally. Look at a person's features and you will know who he is. Our bearing represents our being. You know that when people slump down, they are depressed. But why are they depressed? Negative expectations give rise to negative results, negative results give birth to poor posture that gives birth to nonverbal messages of despair and failure. The body instinctively wants to tell the truth, and it expresses what is inside.

As an example, notice how anger shows in bodily movement. Anger is an expression of the feeling that one is not capable or is trapped and can find no solutions. If you expect failure, you have it. Who of us would do business with or hire an angry person? What a mistake that would be!

A sage once said, "Walk with me and you'll know all the secrets of the world." Walking is a magnetic communion in which what we are is revealed. It works with the magnetic elements of the earth and can heal you and help you grow in prosperity. If you know how to walk, you'll be highly successful in life. We can work on improving our bearing, thereby increasing our confidence, which results in a positive attitude with positive results. These positive results will be perceived by others. Proper bearing releases tremendous energy in our body and creates our own world of prosperity.

C – COMMUNICATION

First, you cannot communicate if you can't think clearly enough to express yourself without misunderstanding. As stated many times in this book, you must first be aware of the thoughts you have and sort out the positive from the negative. Thoughts are like sharp tools; you must know how to use them skillfully. Remember, positive thoughts and expressions, like positive attitudes, render positive results.

Expressing a positive attitude, demonstrating a confident bearing, and conveying in words what positive results you are seeking are the tools of wealth and prosperity. To communicate, your words must first be heard and make sense. You must be able to clearly articulate and pronounce the vowel sounds and consonants precisely. If you have difficulty here, you will be bound to be misunderstood. Lazy people reveal their laziness by slurring word endings. The mentally lethargic commonly use non-words such as "uh" or other pause sounds to buy time mentally. They end up with a jumbled pile of junk words, attempting to string those words together to form an intelligible sentence. This is not clear communication nor is it indicative of a healthy mental state.

Language has been a beautiful and expressive medium for thousands of years. Actually, the further back in time you travel, the more complex and expressive the language. Just consider Koine

Greek, or the common Greek language. There are four words for love, each of which defines the precise "variety" of that love: brotherly love, God's love, etc. In English we have only one word for love. Go back even further to the ancient Sanskrit and you will find one of the most expressive and beautiful of tongues.

It is thought that the ancient Atlantean language was even more expressive and beautiful and that Sanskrit was its guttural offspring. Whatever the case, the people who spoke those beautiful ancient tongues did not use non-sentences like, "Well, ah, um, you know, um, I mean, uh, you know what I mean. Huh?" Or what about, "I'd love to do life with you, but I've got to balance my cosmic blockage so I can ascend to the mother ship's frequency and orchestrate my astral body within parallel lifetimes so that my Master can tune me and beam me up to the 33rd degree of nirvanic enlightenment." Or "Hey! We're doing it with a shaman on Mt. Shasta who gets your kundalini going with the violet flame."

The above examples are seen as crude, vulgar and irrational, which additionally are indicative of pathological states of mental functioning. There

The Moth Comes to the Flame

are two states of being, one exemplified by positive evolution and the other exemplified by degeneration. I believe there will be a consequential extinction of degenerative beings as these two species slide past in opposite directions like mammoth tectonic plates. There will be an "earthquake" of epic proportions when the truth of our genius is communicated honestly and precisely.

Today the question still remains to be answered: Are we simply an updated version of *Homo habilis*, or are we the offspring of the gods, the offspring of pre-Adamic man? Is our speech more reminiscent of the guttural intonations of a prehistoric cave dweller, or is it more reflective of a luminous being whose intelligence is of mammoth proportions? Could it be that some of us are long lost descendants of the early visitors to our blue-green orb? So many who seek communication and contact can't even utter an intelligent sentence in primitive and guttural English.

We can train any bird that flies in the heavens and any beast that wanders in field or forest, so why is it that the tongue is so difficult to train? We appear to have turned our word, our magic wand, into a club with which we bludgeon ourselves.

If you but see the issue that is presented, not only will you have more money but healthier and better relationships and expanded states of consciousness. This leads to greater physical and mental health. First, you must watch your words, both how you use them and what you are really saying. Your speech must be clear and understandable, free of all non-words. Precise articulation, conscious control over the pace or speed at which words are spoken, the power or volume and the tonal pitch, your eye contact and facial expression, physical mannerisms, hand gestures and many other factors, all go into effective communication.

Consider that for thousands of years the salesperson was the highest-paid worker. To this day, not much has changed. Why is a Bill Gates or a Warren Buffett so awesomely wealthy? Is it because they are so much smarter than everyone else? No! It is because they are able to communicate their ideas and are tenacious and persistent in doing so. Some of us choose to use our communication skills for spiritual growth to help speed our return to the garden of truth in the valley of long lost peace. Even the greatest of salesman returns Home once his work is done.

Five Self Sabotages that Prevent Prosperity

Introduction to the Five Sabotages

Many people appear to work hard and really apply themselves, yet success keeps eluding them. This often occurs when people have character traits that are discussed in the five types of sabotage that keep us from wealth.

How Do Rich People Work?

If you despise the rich, you'll never be able to obtain richness because you will not love yourself enough to receive it. John Foster said, "There are two things needed these days: First, for rich people to find out how poor people live; and second, for poor people to know how rich people work."

If you resent wealth in others, you'll never prosper. It is a fact: poor people do not know how rich people work. When people condemn wealth, they are often just condemning virtue. Is it not a virtue to aspire to higher intelligence, better skills, greater talents and abilities? If sharper attention, memory and perception are the attributes of an expanding consciousness, what would be characteristic of a limited scope of consciousness? How about sloth, apathy, a feeling of victimization, impulsiveness, envy and a deep-seated defiance of power or authority? Are we not constantly astounded by the crime rates associated with urban and rural poverty? And yet, in spite of these facts, who of us would be so bold as to say that poverty is nothing more than criminal behavior? And what is it that creates poverty? Isn't it a lack of education, poor work skills, inattention, untrained memory, bad attitude and negative expectations?

Criminal Thought Patterns

The reason people suffer so is that they are unaware of what constitutes criminality. Poverty is no more a blessing than money is the sole indicator of wealth. Wealth is the harmonious application of universal laws in one's life. These laws are clear and defined. They are designed so that all who desire to may become rulers of their reality. What would it mean to your self-esteem and spiritual growth if you were able to identify and apply these laws in your life? There are countless seminars available on this topic and they all have one flaw in common — they do not identify or teach you to recognize criminal thought patterns.

There are five ways we sabotage ourselves. When these traps of thought are discovered and removed, only then are we free to accept wealth as our birthright.

Self-Sabotage #1 — Impulsiveness

The first sabotage leading to poverty is impulsiveness. A criminal, or one with poverty consciousness, embraces impulsivity. Immediate gratification is sought no matter what.

Anything worth having in life is worth building toward. Saving money is much like the functioning of an hourglass; before we realize it, the tiny grains of sand have accumulated. Remember Aesop's fable, "The Grasshopper and the Ant?" Do something to provide for the days to come. The grasshopper wanted to play irresponsibly, knowing that winter would come; then, when there was a shortage, he wanted to sponge off the industrious ant who had saved. The person who is not impulsive, like the ant, has a pocketful of resources. The impulsive person makes decisions based on impulse and emotion rather than reason and facts. Consider people who run up their credit cards far beyond payable limits. This is impulsive buying.

Do you behave reasonably, or do you act on whims without weighing the costs or the consequences of your actions? The criminal mind has an impulsive nature that does something just because they "felt like it." This can be seen as impulsivity toward food, spending, sex or whatever. The cost of their behavior is never considered, and suddenly disaster strikes, seemingly out of the blue.

The enemy is the philosophy that has been embraced: Impulsiveness versus reason. Reason always seeks the facts. The word "clairvoyance" is a French word meaning to see clearly, to see through the haze, seeing the beginning and the end. We want to see clearly, and we do so when we seek reason — when we seek facts.

One study found that people who are in prison have, on average, a ten percent lower IQ than the general population. Their ability to reason clearly was never developed.

Impulsiveness always says, "I want it now; don't tell me about the consequences." The impulsive person suffers from buying what they cannot afford. Inner strength calls for saying yes or no when appropriate. This is true whether it regards appetite or any other issue. Ask, "Is it an addictive, emotional want, or is it rational and life-enhancing?"

One gets out of poverty by making minute-to-minute decisions over a long period of time. Develop discipline and you will find that life rewards discipline with prosperity.

There is a spiritual dimension to prosperity and wealth. Many problems of the world, including poverty, are solved by taking care of one's self and one's business. Take care of those you are responsible for, and then there will be no one needing to be taken care of by the government, society or the church.

Extortion in any form is robbery. Our current beliefs that we must give to the have-nots by robbing those who have through taxation and the complexities of law come from a philosophy that is communistic. History abounds with the results of such thinking. All end in revolution and destruction. For a nation to prosper, we must give abundantly out of our own free will, not through a law of extortion.

People who live in poverty expect help and believe they are "entitled," but remember, so did the grasshopper in Aesop's fable. This does not rule out the law of compassion. Compassionate and loving beings do not ask the world to give them anything they can create for themselves. Compassionate, loving people give privately and in secret. The moral community helps those in need one-on-one. If it is not a moral community, no amount of law, taxation or coercion can correct it.

Wealth: Five Self-Sabotages that Prevent Prosperity

Decent people will always give because their hearts have been touched. Be responsible to yourself and to your neighbor who is deserving, but not to those who are needy and demanding entitlement. It is fine to give. What is being said is that it is as unconscionable to legislate that people give as it is to be robbed by tears.

Like the parable of the ant and the grasshopper, people didn't do what they knew they needed to do and now they want to be provided for. Some are impulsive and overextend themselves, and then want to receive from others who did save. The government often legislates that those who saved — like the ant — must be taxed to pay for those who were impulsive—like the grasshopper.

Rather than being impulsive and succumbing to the first sabotage, become wise and be enriched as you learn from your experiences so you do not repeat the same mistakes over and over again. Do not become a conspirator in crimes against yourself. Guard against impulsive behavior in your life. Look at the areas where you tend to be impulsive and think them through. Understand that all actions have consequences.

Life does not come from material items alone, though we all deserve the opportunity to create good food and comfortable housing. No one forces us to behave negatively. We choose.

Self-Sabotage #2 — An Anti-Mind, Anti-Thinking Attitude

Those who are against thinking and use of the mind have a poverty mentality and, not infrequently, a criminal mentality. Just examine the consequences of certain actions, and you can determine whether the decisions that led to them were enhancing or negating.

It's fine to use intuition. That is not anti-mind, particularly when we recognize that intuition stands for the "in tutor," the teacher inside of us. Intuition means a lightning bolt of reason. It is the ability to draw from the unconsciousness rational patterns of past solutions and apply them to the present situation. It is a "conscious unconsciousness."

A lot of people just don't want to think because it requires energy, but without thinking we will always be in poverty. People who are anti-mind have a hard time remembering names because it requires mental energy to listen and to hear the name in the first place. Many impoverished communities exemplify an attitude of anti-mind. Though a simplified statement, the criminal elements and rowdy gang-like groups in schools tend to demonstrate a distaste for studiousness.

Anti-mind people don't explore issues, and the lack of communication leads to numerous problems in relationships. When people cannot communicate, frustration boils over and becomes anger. The goal is to see both sides of an issue objectively. Anti-mind people do not admire intelligence or accomplishment.

Admire intelligence and you will become intelligent. People who use their minds prosper. There is a gap that is ever widening between those who do and those who do not use their minds. Like it or not, in a democratic nation this is defined as rich and poor.

Prosperity may be defined as the state of those who can utilize, hold onto, and properly cultivate wealth in terms of happiness, contentment and well-being. Wealth also encompasses the ability to communicate and prosper in relationships.

To survive in these fast-paced days, one must utilize and develop the mind. You must learn how to think clearly or your mind will be on automatic, subject to programming by the environment and others. Life is magical for the person who can think clearly.

Self-Sabotage #3 — Defiance of Authority

People who feel victimized are usually in defiance of authority. Defiance of authority keeps people from being prosperous and contributes to criminality. People who are in defiance of authority are those who say they are not going to do certain activities for employment or that they are not being treated fairly. They will say that they do not sweep floors, do windows and on and on. This person feels victimized and is ready to jump up and fight.

An example of this was seen in the Rodney King incident in Los Angeles. The police were frustrated and Rodney King was defiant. With those ingredients the outcome was predictable, but two wrongs never make a right. It was a crime involving a moral issue between Rodney King and the police, but because people were feeling victimized in that area of Los Angeles, they burned down other people's buildings and looted them. In people's minds, this perception of being victimized justified their criminal behavior.

Victims volunteer to be fired through their actions — they teach authority figures how to treat them. When you go to work for someone, you are offering yourself to get a certain job done. If you don't submit to your employer's authority, you won't keep the job; it's quite simple.

You have to earn your right to have the authority, and this only comes with accepting more responsibility. When people earn the right to authority, and we defy that right, we are setting ourselves up for self-sabotage. We may not agree with that authority, but as long as we agree to contract with it, it *is* the authority.

The criminal element of society doesn't want to hold up to their end of the contract. Holding a job is essential for acquiring creature comforts.

The Moth Comes to the Flame

You learn how to swallow your ego and petty gripes and work toward the position you want, but the self-sabotaging mind does not understand this.

The person in a position of authority is not always ethical, but they have earned the right to issue the commands. You can present your opinions if they differ, but one must always know who the boss is. When you go to work, you should consider that you are, in effect, always self-employed even when working for someone else. You will still create your own circumstances internally.

You are, in fact, employed by the divine. That is, your returns are in direct relationship to your application of the spiritual laws. So now *really* go to work for the company you work for.

Attitude and bearing are important to employment. Negative, complaining people get picked on, are grouchy and have lousy body language. The weakest emotionally will always get picked on.

With changes in our economy looming on the horizon, there will be a lot of people without jobs.

The old saying goes, "Hire the best, fire the rest." So if you're not with the best, you'll be with the rest. The best understand the need for authority; the only way they arrive at that station in life is not by defying, but by respecting, authority; then when they have it, they handle it responsibly.

Self-Sabotage #4 — Amorality

Amorality is an indicator of criminality and poverty. Amorality is the lack of morality. Morality is associated with choice. There are laws of social convention and then there are universal principles which give rise to what we call morality. What is beneficial and good for you is moral. What benefits your life is good. What does not benefit your life is bad.

Morality is the standard you've arrived at, based on your own choices. Morality entails long-term commitment to a plan to make those virtues your own.

The criminal mind is not willing to make a long-term commitment to growth. People who live in poverty don't make long-term commitments to their growth either. Both groups feel they have no choices. Both criminal and poverty-conscious individuals are fatalistic, feeling their circumstances are a result of their fate or destiny.

You can choose your reality, your destiny. Amorality in the criminal's behavior is often without regret or conscience, as they see themselves as apart from their actions. They do not see that their behavior has been unproductive or harmful to themselves and others. As an example, stealing at the workplace is not an issue to them, nor is cheating on their mate or lying. But this is immoral because it violates trust and honesty on all levels.

You are not helpless in the hands of destiny. You always have choices. What makes your life better and what makes it worse? You can always replace a wrong choice with a right choice.

Quit looking for the comfortable paradise. Become comfortable with the struggle before you. We do struggle, but we can accept where we are. Apply energy and effort. Develop sufficient attention to concentrate.

When we are moral, we are making the choices that are good for us and others in the long term. There are no outside laws, no list of someone else's do's and don'ts, but there is an inside law, a law of conscience, and divine law dictates moral conduct. What is not moral is not good for you.

We always have choices before us. There is the seed of light and the seed of darkness, the wheat and the weeds. One offers a richness, the other emptiness. One produces, the other does not.

As the parable goes, the weed and wheat will grow together until the time of harvest, when there will be a separation of those who are productive from those who are not.

Those who walk in the light will be just fine. Make long-term commitments to your growth, to your physical bodies, health, strength and mind. Focus on your spirit, your essence. The commitment to this type of growth will continue through this lifetime and even pick up later in another. Longevity is needed so we can hang around long enough to do what we love and to serve our purpose.

When you love life, life loves you, and it becomes luminous and joyous. When you start to get rich and full, you bow your head to life and to the light. That life and its source is what we worship.

Self-Sabotage #5 — Victimization

This is the "you won't believe what happened to me" mentality. This starts in early childhood when some children learn to get more attention by hurting themselves than by achievement or other positive behaviors. They don't realize that they are not only victims, but also unconscious volunteers for a disastrous life.

Feeling victimized is one of the indicators of both poverty and criminality. The feeling of being victimized is the "poor me" attitude. When we are exhibiting qualities of victimization, we feel victimized, along with a corresponding righteous indignation. Criminality and poverty have similar qualities. When we are offended, we are feeling like a victim. Frequently, segments of the society begin to feel offended over financial issues.

Wealth: Five Self-Sabotages that Prevent Prosperity

Criminals are crude materialists and feel victimized when they don't get what they think they deserve. Others of impoverished mentality believe in entitlement, that the government owes money or a certain level of comfort to them. When you ask a person who is living in victim consciousness to pay their own way, they bristle and take offense.

Though many decent, non-impoverished, non-criminal people enjoy solitude, there is a tendency for criminals to be loners even though they may appear to run in gangs. To be reclusive does not mean one is a criminal, but combined with other tendencies, it begins to create a pattern that points to victim consciousness. Being reclusive is desirable at times, but to be antisocial and to pull away because of the fear of victimization is a criminal tendency.

If you fear being victimized, you won't help others. The rational person knows that helping others get what they want will always motivate others to help him get what he wants.

Eliminate Impoverished Behavior

It is important to recognize the criminal or impoverished behavior in ourselves and eliminate those tendencies. If we get offended easily, that is criminal behavior. It is also impoverished behavior because it impoverishes our lives. Being easily frustrated is both a criminal and impoverished characteristic, as is having no long-term goals.

In raising the five red flags, we are suggesting that these are *some* of the indicators; they are not indicative in and of themselves. At certain times, all of us may display the red flags, but if these begin to rise repeatedly and accumulate, there is increasing likelihood of impoverished and criminal mentality and activity.

PETER'S PROSPERITY TIPS

1. Let your close association be only with thankful, appreciative people, who know how to say "thank you," and ask nothing in return.

2. Never ever listen to the whiner or the complainer. If you do, you may begin to feel that the world is unjust and unfair. The complainer throws hot coals into your eyes, and blinds you to the beauty and richness that is yours. Avoid them like the plague.

3. Associate only with people who follow through, those whose word is their honor. People who do not do what they say, are dishonest. Dishonesty breeds poverty on all levels of being.

4. End each day by writing all the blessings you have incurred that day; all the reasons to say "thank you." You will sleep sweetly and richly. Your night will be a continuous affirmation of prosperity.

5. Make beauty your god, and worship it in everything you see, feel and experience. Then your life will be beautiful, peaceful and rich. Remember, ugliness becomes beauty when you see the reason for contrast. The star shines brighter because the night is dark.

6. Do not envy others, for to do so is to only affirm your own lack. If you envy others, you are only saying "poor me." So be it... you have two wishes left!

7. Rejoice and celebrate others' successes. For some, this may appear difficult, and yet this is another overlooked universal law. You will never be successful until you love success in others.

8. Let your self-talk be free of condemnation. Learn from your mistakes, and forget them. That's why pencils have erasers on them. If you focus on your so-called mistakes, remember, you get what you set!

Wealth: Five Self-Sabotages that Prevent Prosperity

9. Value time — spend it wisely. Don't allow others to steal it with trivia. Many people have lots of time, while other people have lots of money. The prosperous person has both.

10. You must be rich inside first if outer richness is to have any meaning. You will only become rich outside by enriching the lives of others. You will only become rich inside when you can understand what real value is all about. Never confuse glass with diamonds... a few diamonds go a long way!

PETER'S PROSPERITY TIPS were also included in The Fruit of Your Thoughts. *Their significance justifies repeating them in this book.*

Generosity

Generosity Returns Tenfold

Sincere generosity returns tenfold and more; tenfold returns produce one hundredfold results. Yet, be aware that often we are intimidated into a false generosity by allowing ourselves to be taken advantage of by other people's tears. Your integrity cannot be held ransom by another's needs. Give to people you choose, from the sincere recesses of your heart. Altruism is different from kindness. When you feel you must give to every single person to prove yourself worthy, it is not kindness. Do be kind, but understand that altruism means that you value others, even total strangers, more than yourself. Never give just to get someone else's approval; that showy display is hollow and impotent.

Authentic generosity returns to the giver and creates a double-win situation. With altruism, the receiver is the winner and the only thing the giver gets is a little sob for his misguided conscience.

Give From Your Abundance

There is great truth in giving ten percent as people do who practice tithing, but you must never try to buy approval. The question is, who are you giving the ten percent to? Are they worthy? Are you seeking to buy approval or are you giving from your abundance? Are you giving from abundance because of the joy you feel? If you enjoy giving just because it tickles your heart, don't stop with 10 percent. Let your giving be an appreciation, not a set amount.

Tip for good service and tip extra well for extra-good service. Be a very generous person. You can never go wrong because generosity has to return. It is just the way it is. What you sow you reap. We create our realities wherever we go.

Give because you appreciate something. The motive is everything. We give, not just in money, but in smiles and kind words as well as how we treat others. Great people treat lesser people royally. Find ways to tell people how much you appreciate them.

So often your giving is privately enjoyed, and warms your heart like a fireplace full of crackling logs on a winter night. No one need know your private joy.

When you love to give, and give cheerfully, it comes back ten times over and more.

Spirituality

The Nature of God

Where Is God?

A man was walking with his young son one day. The father was emotionally distraught, feeling totally depressed about life. When they stopped by a wall, the father scrawled in graffiti: God is nowhere.

The young boy had just recently learned to read and write. He looked at what his father had written and said, "Daddy, you didn't write it correctly." Then he wrote his correction: God is now here.

It is our choice whether we see God as "nowhere," or God as "now here."

Where Are You Looking?

Where are you looking for God? People look for God in all the wrong places. The prime mover is discovered when the artist becomes the painting and the dancer becomes the dance. God is in the beauty of all creation.

There is a story of a master, an artist-sage who was sipping mulberry wine out of a beautiful ceramic cup. A young man came along and asked him, "What is the Tao?," meaning, of course, what is God? The master sage said, "I don't know; I've been too busy enjoying it."

How can you not drink of God if God is everywhere?

Look into your own eyes and ask, "Who is the true seer?" In time you will discover it is God. God cannot hide because God is everywhere. God cannot be limited. You may look for God in mythical heavens or in mystical places, but God is in your eyes and heart and feet and brain and even in your dog (which is god spelled backwards).

It's a wonderful experience for someone to say, "I know you. I see the God in your eyes." It is this God in you that makes you able to laugh when tested, to endure when tired and to love in the face of rejection.

See God in Beauty

What really brings you bliss? For me, it is seeing God in beauty everywhere. When your God's name is Beauty, you can worship it anywhere, even in the midst of the ghetto, in the old junkyard dog and in the dandelions growing from the cracks in the concrete.

When you worship beauty, you worship God. God is in all matter — in the wind, the snow, the sun and the people reading these words. Where you find beauty, you find God.

Jesus had to deal with people who, for generations, had been taught strict religious practices for reaching God. Jesus worshipped truth and loved all kinds of people and found beauty everywhere. He asked, "Have you not heard that you are gods?" (John 10:34) Jesus came with the energy of life in abundance and the love of life and truth and of facts. In fact, try this yourself: Where you find beauty, look carefully and you will find God.

The Universe Is Within You

Krishna's mother looked inside baby Krishna's mouth and saw the sun and the stars and all that shined. This is just a way of saying that within us is all that shines. You get it all when you find out Who is inside. Then you can live the exceptional life.

God's Will Is Your Deepest Will for Yourself

What is your will for yourself? If you can tell me that, then I can tell you what God's will is for you. The divine sculptor is God. His divine energy does not want us to suffer but to create, in like image, a beautiful world where there is peace. Where there is peace there is beauty, and where there is beauty there is God, and love abounds.

The God-self is our illuminated self which knows what we truly want deeply within our own hearts.

It knows how to succeed at this game of life. A great sage said, "My God is beauty. I see it wherever I go. I see it everywhere."

Why do we spend time looking at the sky when everything we are seeking is in our midst? Taste it and see how you like it. God is to be experienced, but we have been conditioned to use the mind to conceive of God. God is not a telling; God is an experience. "Be still and know that I am God." When you have this ability to be still, you are in control of your universe.

God cannot hide because God is everywhere.

QUESTIONS AND ANSWERS

How can one avoid distractions that tend to pull us away from the spiritual path?

There is a saying that "The seeker must be in the world but not of the world." This means the seeker must always be centered within the self, or put another way, always identifying with the part that is watching or witnessing the events within the illusionary world around him. That is why the East uses the symbol of the lotus flower. The lotus comes from the mud but grows until it raises itself above the very water of the pond that gave it roots and life. Then, it flowers.

We too must raise ourselves above our own muddy roots and the childlike world of colored lights, toys and magical illusions. We must raise ourselves to the pinnacle of clairvoyance, which means clear sight. When we have cleansed our eyes with the rain of a million tears, we suddenly discover our fruitless desires have led us down "the wrath-begotten path, all consuming, ever looming. This the enemy ever booming..." road of despair.

The distraction and the deception are the same. The childlike, illusionary belief that one more toy, one more new experience, one more sensation will lead to peace eternal is a false hope.

The sage is born in the moment, the sudden explosive moment of realization that happiness, fulfillment and peace are properties of the inner realm alone. Thus the sage immerses himself deeply in meditation on his interior world and its profoundly unspeakable treasures. It is here, for the sage, that his world begins.

By contrast, the seeker is seeking in too many directions at the same time. The seeker can be easily deceived by the fancy of his eye, the counterfeit appearance of serenity and peace exhibited by jet-setting to the ends of the earth, or the insatiable quest for wealth and fame.

Personally, I have never met a person who has had enough money, power, sensation or security in his life other than an enlightened being who has become impervious to distraction by the external world. The sage considers the world foolish in its pursuits, as foolish as someone chasing his own shadow or running to find the illusionary pot of gold at the end of the rainbow.

How wise the counsel, "Seek first the kingdom and its righteousness (right-use-ness), and all these other things will be added unto you." (Matthew 6:33). Where is this kingdom and its treasure? In the world? No! When Jesus rebuked the religious leaders of his day they were standing and pointing to the stars and heavens. Jesus said, "The kingdom you seek is in your heart." And I say, if you have attached and stuck your heart on vain fancies, you will forever seek it in vain. Go deep within your interior house and you will find the abode your Father has prepared for you from the beginning of time.

Ah, if not, the seeker seeks in vain. Even the words of his guide fall on deaf ears. Some may protest this, but beliefs do not erase facts. Just look at how easily one falls prey to distressing news or gossip. It only shows that the outside world of flickering lights has more power over that soul than the inside world, the treasure-house of consciousness and eternal peace.

Just go within and discover reality and you'll never be distracted again. How? First you must practice detachment and ask without ceasing, "Who is the seer? Who is seeing and what is seeing?" Suddenly, one day by surprise, the master speaks and distractions dissolve. Then the prayer, "Lord, lead me not into temptation" will have been answered forevermore, and you will have returned to your Father's house, never to stray again.

Masters and Mastery

The Man Who Fell into a Well

There once was a man who fell into a well. Another man came along and reached his hand down to pull him out. The man in the well looked up and asked, "Who are you?"

The man said, "I am a friend."

The man in the well said, "Never mind. I don't want to be saved by a friend."

So the man, trying to be helpful, said, "Then I am a stranger."

The man in the well, who was nearly drowning by now, asked, "Why have you come to help then?"

The man, still trying to assist, said, "I was sent by God." The drowning man stated he did not want to be saved by God.

Finally the rescuer said, "I am a master."

"Oh," said the drowning man, "then pull me out of here."

The man didn't want to be saved by a friend because all of his friends were drowning in the sea of life just as he was — and so were the strangers. Metaphorically, he could not be saved by someone like himself. He also didn't want to be saved by God because God is not the flower but the fragrance. A fragrance couldn't reach down and pull him up. But through a master, God's fragrance could manifest. The fragrance, which is God, enriches everything.

Become Master of Your Own Universe

The new teaching is that we are not here to wallow in misery and servitude, but to become masters of the universe. We are the initiators of the cause. We are not helpless victims.

When you learn deeply and completely the law of cause and effect, you have learned to master your destiny here on Earth. Knowing that you are in control of your reality is your only ticket to freedom. Being out of control is the greatest nightmare and leads to every manner of confinement.

A master's greatest adventure is found quietly sitting on his porch watching the flowers growing by themselves while the insane crowd races nervously and restlessly, clamoring for the next new sight to satiate their dull and lifeless eyes and dried-up withered souls.

They (the crowd) are never home and never will be. They (the crowd) are more cursed than Sisyphus endlessly pushing the stone of toil up the mountain of agony, for the crowd is doomed by destiny to be more like dumb beasts chasing carrots through the corridors of eternity, eating and purging forever in their search for fun. Every choice is but a decision to think a certain thought which manifests as an action which results in the circumstances that weave the fabric of our destiny.

Peter says, "When you have authentic mastery, your tastes and desires change. You live life in simple elegance and seek more and more quietude. With mastery you are content to watch the sunrises and sunsets for there is rich fulfillment in such simplicities."

You Can Be the Master of Your Destiny

We will learn only when we become wise. We have choices all around us. Every step we take is another new choice.

Choose life so that you can be blessed from this point onward. We can do anything when we want to do it. Light, joy, peace and happiness — this is our inheritance and we must choose it over and over again!

Become your own proof. You must discover what your destiny is. Others can only point a finger in certain directions. You must determine if the direction is right for you. Do whatever you need to do until you get to the point where you are leading a conscious and loving life. Be careful! Whatever you truly want, wants you. This is an amazing discovery. You always get the fulfillment of your deepest subconscious desires, and they are usually not the surface desires of which you are superficially aware.

Let No One Make You a Slave

Hold your own high values and help others around you. Eliminate self-doubt and see things in a really conscious manner. Seek awareness in all things. Who knows, you may just live the luminous life forever — and keep your body, too!

Miracles Are Unexplained Natural Laws

Miracles are really natural laws that we do not always understand. There is no miracle that does not have a cause.

Magic is not without a cause. Envision what you want and it is likely to become reality. If your focus is extremely powerful, miracles can be developed by concentration and meditation exercises. Miracles are natural laws in action.

Visualize what you want and at a subtle level, it starts to form. When the first visible evidence occurs, it affirms your vision, and it begins to pick up speed.

Living masters provide us with role models.

Move Through Life with Grace

How would a god walk, talk and sit down? How would a god deal with finances and health? What kind of clothing would be worn, and what kind of food would be eaten by a god? We can only speculate; however, if you're fortunate enough to observe a living master, then you will know.

If one can live luminously and successfully, then there is hope for all to do so. Living masters show us the way by being models. What are the traits and habits of such a person?

Role models of successful living come in the form of evolved beings, people who truly shine. They model how to master our health, money and emotional circumstances. Lighthearted people are not artificial, but are often artistic, poetic and animated with spirit and zeal. They are not so much amusing as they are amazing. They do not see life as awful but as awe-filled.

One of the differences between what can be called a "Shining One" and an ordinary mortal is the brightness of the aura. The Shining Ones have "brighter lights." Their auras are bright and their physical bodies carry a perfection. It requires a clear spiritual sight to see them. Their thoughts are chosen carefully.

The Touch of the Master's Hand

You can be molded by a master's hand. You are being touched by the master's hand when you seek life at its best.

Do you know the qualities of a real master? Is there one with all those qualities right before you, but you find yourself running off, still looking?

If you find a teacher, a friend, a master, do not discount them easily. Do not get caught up in the habit of searching without really searching, of searching without being aware. We tend to make a habit of looking without really expecting to find.

Pointing to the Moon

A master would give you the moon if he could. But the master can only point to the moon, he cannot give it to you. You must earn it for yourself. The gift of the master is in his reflection of the light that points out "the moon" to you. The master's hand can only point and say, "This is what I do." Follow and make your experiences your own. Experiment and test and learn what is life-affirming and consciousness-expanding.

What a voyage it is! Just sitting or walking with awareness becomes a sacred privilege. It can only be pointed to. It cannot be taught.

The Scent of the Master

Sometimes a master will have a scent of frankincense and myrrh which is the combination of peace and love. When the mind is clear, the body becomes clear and clean also.

The Master Is a Laundryman Who Washes Our Hearts Inside Out

We come into this world pure, white and bright; but over time, our minds accumulate dust and become gray with stains. The stains of life come from the pains of life. So the master comes and washes and irons and gives the pureness back to our original forms. We come to this life to re-find (refine) our purity. We can be refined by a master.

A Master Dispels Darkness

If we would learn how to think, we would not need armies, politics or gurus. The job of the guru would be to have no disciples. A teacher's role is to dispel the darkness and guide others into living consciously. *Gu* + *ru* means to dispel the dark. A master teacher knows what we are thinking and can enter our dreams and then tell us about them. They do not tell us what to do but may ask if we've thought of looking at something this way or that way.

Since electrical charges travel through the ethers and thoughts are electrical, a teacher can hold loving thoughts and affect the person he is thinking about from any distance. We are all teachers and can exchange healing by having loving thoughts rather than fearful or judgmental ones.

When you feel love, others will sense your electromagnetic field and feel safe around you. Cleansing the negative thoughts creates a harmonious field of attraction.

Everything embraced by love grows. If you are not loved, you will not live. Love yourself and others will find you lovable.

The intentions of the teacher count. Intentions get results. What are your intentions and how are they manifesting results in your life? You are both the student and the teacher to those who follow in your wake. Hold the master's hand and walk along by his side and perhaps one day you will be his equal. It is an open invitation. If you trust the master that much, he promises to never hurt you and never let you get hurt. Friendship does not come back unfulfilled.

Be a Disciple of Life

To be a disciple, to discipline oneself, is to learn from all that is around you. Don't just know about things, be them. Disciples of life know why they hold certain beliefs. They have challenged their unexamined beliefs, which all too often had become like concrete — mixed up and firmly set.

You must show your mastery before masters will be interested in you. Master your reality. Be one less person who needs saving. Make sure you're not needy. Masters love helping those who are conscientious and sincere. Go out, work, and they will be there to help you. Masters are in love with your spiritual accomplishments, energy and awareness.

You teach what you know. To be a real teacher is very difficult; you have to know something first. The real teacher says, "Look at this" or "Look at that." Then try it out and see if it helps your life.

Somewhere a Dreamer Is Ready to Wake

When spirit blazes in our hearts, the flames get kindled, and the dross burns away. Life chisels, hammers and bangs at us while the grand sculptor is working. Everyone else is here so that we can see a reflection of our own beauty. You are the only actor. All the others are stand-ins in this life, and they help us see how we will respond, how we will be responsible (response-able).

Apprentices on the Path Are Not Servants

Worship all that is heroic in people. Ours is the path of the hero. Apprentices make their own decisions and don't wait, like servants, for someone to make decisions for them. Personal responsibility is the watchword of the apprentice. Apprentices are happy people and are in control of their destiny. They know that their thoughts are illuminated with energy and create their world.

Are you happy, healthy, successful and prosperous? If so, you've probably taken one thought at a time and focused on it. The servant waits for someone to do it for him, whereas the apprentice on the path of life holds positive thoughts in concentrated form and reaches superconscious states.

The apprentice learns to concentrate. It has been said that when he holds that concentrative state for approximately twelve minutes, meditation takes place, and when he can hold that meditative state approximately twelve minutes, superconsciousness takes place. When he can hold superconsciousness for another twelve minutes, enlightenment occurs.

Everything embraced by love grows.

A Master Knows Who You Are

Masters know who you are only because they know themselves so well that the self has faded from sight; and there you are, standing there like an old lost friend, in all your glory. When you know the scent, you know where to find the luminous ones. The right opportunity, time and place will arrive for those who have the courage to live the life of freedom. The masters have known us for a very long time.

When you become aware, you will find that others may not hear the birds sing or see the grass glisten or catch a waft of perfume on a gentle breeze, but you will. The master goes his way with tears in his eyes.

You can become more real
than you ever dreamed you could be.
Let your awareness be touched by
memories of long ago: one fire, one heart.
One on one, we will light
each other's spirits in remembering.

QUESTIONS AND ANSWERS

What is a master?

A master is not a grieving mirror. The cat has already walked by.

Okay, Peter. Thanks for the haiku. I will ponder that one.

That's not a haiku, John.

You speak about Aristotle, Bodhidharma, Buddha, Jesus, Diogenes and many others. Do they not contradict each other?

Certainly. As many minds as there are, John, that's how many contradictions you will find, but these men do not contradict goodness from my definition of the word good. Since I love these great teachers so much, I have been able to find a common thread and have woven their truths into the fabric of my own personal experience. When Jesus said, "You will know the truth and the truth will set you free," he must have sounded more like a Greek than a Jew. In fact, many very solid assertions have been made indicating Jesus may have been none other than Apollonius of Tyana, the Greek Messiah, who was said to have been put to death on a cross. If you were to examine his teachings, you would be hard-pressed to tell the difference.

In 130 A.D., Marcion, who was later called Mark, recorded and translated these words in Greek and Latin which are said to be the basis of the New Testament. The Book of Mark is, as many biblical scholars state, the oldest text, and the one translated as the Codex

Vaticanus *and* Codex Sinaiticus *in the 4th century A.D. They acknowledge that the authors of Matthew and Luke each adopted the Gospel of Mark, though, admittedly, in a slightly different manner. Another school of theological research has concluded that the* Rylands Papyrus *(known as P52) was the oldest extant fragment of the New Testament. It contains a few verses of John and is dated no later than A.D. 150. Now the question of what the truth is remains. How can one determine truth?*

Remember, there is a difference between a claim and a truth. Knowledge of a claim and a reason why it is true require the examination of a premise. A premise is a proposition supporting a conclusion. So one must ask, "On what does this rest?" You cannot conclude something is true without examining beliefs. Solid facts are needed, and beliefs do not erase the facts. Facts are discovered by reason. Is there any substance? Substance requires both quantity and quality. When we understand what it is for us to be a substance, then we begin to understand what it is to exist. When our knowledge becomes experience, truth is revealed. Then this truth is incon-

testably valid. When your life is an experience of truth, you are freed from fables.

I love the liberated and awakened Being. That is why I speak about those you just mentioned, about Aristotle, Bodhidharma, Buddha, Jesus and Diogenes. Their personal experiences of truth gave them wings to fly to the Father of all substance. May we all have the courage to follow.

A friend asks, "What is an Ascended Master? You urge us to test for the truth. How can we 'test' this? Are we supposed to find or contact one? What exactly is meant by 'ascended?'"

First, the word must be understood. An ascendant is a position of dominance, an increase in power. To ascend is to succeed to a high position, such as a throne. It also means a gradual, upward movement. I often hesitate to even discuss the topic, due to the incredible insanity, hallucination and lunacy associated with it. Any nut can make an arbitrary claim about anything. If a person tells you they had a dream about little purple men from Mars, are you going to argue that they might really be from Venus? Only a person who has a BB for a brain would ever be caught in such absurd nonsense. An arbitrary claim, by its very nature, requires no answer. I categorically disassociate myself from any and all organizations that the public knows about, that rally round the flag of make-believe ascended masters. I endorse none of their books or irrational postulations.

Anything said by a master to a servant is bound to be misunderstood due to the very nature of their relative positions; and thus, by its nature, is discounted from the realm of discussion.

One must always examine the premise to see if there is any foundation at all for any claim. If there is none, then dismiss it, and don't waste your time on speculation. If there is some concrete, solid, visible, measurable evidence, then you may inquire as to its importance in your life. If one is looking for a master to come and shoulder personal responsibility, the search is in vain. And why else would most people seek one out? To have them tell you, "You are responsible; now what are you going to do about it?" You ask, "Are you supposed to find or contact one?" My reply is, "How could you?" It is only when you have learned to play the music of life with your human instrument to a high degree that you might be invited to play in concert. Until then...

While I rarely use the term "ascended," it refers to an upward elevated state of consciousness. On the ladder of consciousness, attention, memory, awareness, concentration and meditation are the rungs that must be climbed in our everyday, ordinary lives. In the house of Being, no room is unexplored, no doors are without keys.

In Eastern terminology, one has ascended from the maya mano kosha *to the* atmic *form and beyond.* Gate, gate, paragate, Bodhisattva. *Someone may accuse me of making an arbitrary claim by introducing a mental body and a vehicle of soul into the discussion, and rightly so since I speak of a terrain of a relatively unknown land. Let us then confine the answer to personal mastership in a physical world. That means mastery of time, mind, body, money and emotions. Our journey of ascension can begin with what we have before us today. Our lives are like diamonds in the rough. We have an entire lifetime to polish its many facets. But a lifetime goes very fast. So don't waste time on fairy tales and daydreams. Begin today and climb high and then one day, perhaps...*

Many people have testified to your amazing ability to literally pull information about them seemingly out of the air. How do you do that? Does this ability relate to your mastery of concentration and meditation?

It really has as much to do with concentration as it does with meditation, though meditation gives one far greater insight and a greater grasp as to events and historical perspectives about the individual.

When you are able to concentrate on an individual without being distracted by your own head or thoughts, you then can observe the things that make them comfortable or uncomfortable. As an example, if you're giving someone a reading and you mention something about finances and they sit very calmly, then you mention something about romance and they wiggle in their chair, you're alert enough to observe that when you mention this topic the person gets uncomfortable. If you focus your questions around the area of romance, it's very easy to grab hold of a little thread. As you begin to pull that thread with your questions, soon you'll start to get glimpses and mental images in your own head that aren't visible signs before you but are subtle, invisible signs. As you begin to focus on them, they become pictures, and these pictures become dramas. All you have to do is relate what you see. It's as simple as that.

Concentration is the key to focusing on them rather than your own thoughts and daydreams, your own preconceived ideas and judgments. If you can free yourself from those things, then it is easy to tell what the other person is thinking, what the other person is feeling, where the other person has been and where they are going in the future.

Even in my work with police departments, John, one of the things I do is what is called psychometry. In psychometry, you hold an object and get vibrations or sensations from it, but you must be able to concentrate on the object first because the vibrations are so subtle. It is so much a part of the ethers that picking up the sense of an object is like a bloodhound sticking its nose into the air to pick up a most subtle scent. It is much this same way that I use my abilities to concentrate and pick up the "scent" or sense vibration of another.

One day the local police department handed me a black-and-white photograph of a crime scene. In the photograph there were some old, black plastic bags which held, though not visible, a decomposed body. From focusing on the photo I began to be able to reconstruct the person who had been killed. I said that the woman was 5' 7" tall, weighed 145 lbs. and had brown hair and brown eyes. I stated that she came from a wealthy family and that the clothes she wore were purchased in a certain city, which happened to be Atlanta, Georgia, in this instance.

All of these things that would seemingly be impossible to reconstruct were validated by the forensic anthropology laboratory at the university nearby. In a double-blind experiment, they constructed a wax image of the face and body from their scientific approach, and I drew a picture of the person on paper. The two matched perfectly. That which I was able to get from an indistinguishable photograph they were able to come up with through their forensic techniques.

The question is, how did I know that? Well, the entire universe is filled with information, it's just that our heads are so crowded, so busy, so confused and so competitive with the thoughts and opinions of other people that we're never quite clear enough to see what's before us.

I want to emphasize that we have an amazing universe, which goes far beyond our thoughts and is available to us. We reach into that universe by using the laws of concentration. Concentration can lead to a breakthrough in meditation and then meditation into superconsciousness. This is an example of mastery utilizing the laws of the universe.

Can a person master destiny in one lifetime?

If you mean destiny as a preordained fate, bear in mind that karma or destiny does not mean that all events are specifically predetermined and inevitable. If that were the case, you could not ask the question. How could one master what was predetermined and inevitable? So first, a glimpse into karma. Karma refers to and calls for general conditions to prevail so that specific energies may be engaged and thus balanced by the encounter. Every cause must be balanced by an effect. Even if the effect is a long time in coming, even requiring lifetimes to manifest. There are three types of karma traditionally referred to in Eastern texts. First are the causes and effects of your last life (whether you believe in karma or not, we exhibit certain tendencies from birth). Second, the causes we have set in motion during this life. Third, the rather rapid cascade of daily events that can be quickly related to obvious causes during everyday activities.

An example: You choose to stay up later than normal knowing you must get up early for work. The next morning you oversleep, so you drive faster than you should. You cut in front of someone else's car, and they blow their horn loudly, gesture violently, and shout harsh expletives. In your frustration and anger you race away, only to discover flashing blue lights in your rear view mirror. Well, when you finally show up on the job, your boss snaps at you for tardiness. Needless to say, we all can figure out how the rest of the workday unfolds. As you reach the steps to your front door, you notice the cat reacting to your angry mood as it sprays the door. Before the cat can get away, you give it a swift kick. By the way, the wife was looking out the window. You enter the kitchen and she slams down a frozen dinner and tells you to fix it yourself and put the kids to bed by nine; she's going to her mother's. The wife leaves with a good hard slam of the front door. Now, as soon as the mother hears this all-too-familiar story, she replies, "Why don't you just leave the bastard!"

A month passes. You have made up and are invited to a friend's home for dinner. As you are sitting there relaxing and engaging in the small talk of dinner conversation, the host's dog brush-

es against your leg. You reach down to affectionately pet the dog when suddenly, for no apparent reason, the dog nips you and races off. The lords of karma laugh and say, "That one's for the cat! Next?"

So how could this man have avoided this avalanche of despair? What if he had been more conscious at the start of our scenario? What if he had exercised greater restraint of his emotions, greater discipline, greater willpower? What if he was more detached about the effects set in motion? What if he displayed unconditional love through all these little vicissitudes?

This is how to master the karma of day-to-day life. Do that first and then the karma of this lifetime will be worked out. And as far as the bag of debt carried from other lifetimes... hmm... all I can say is, "love burns karma."

Mastery in one lifetime? Yes, it certainly happens. And in some future, present moment, it will happen to everyone. Perhaps the real question you have asked is, "Will it happen for me?" How do you arrive on the other shore without the ferryman and his boat? The question is only, "How far have you traveled on your own?" Have you arrived at my dock? I am here and the boat is my experience.

Meditation

Meditation Is an Experience of Aliveness

All things experienced with consciousness become meditations. Let everything you do in this life be sacred and every act spiritual. All that we do is a worship of life.

If you are going to meditate, first understand why you want to and what it's all about for you. There needs to be a reason. What do you want to receive from meditation? Don't seek unconsciousness but rather seek more consciousness. Meditation is not hypnosis nor is it a paralysis of awareness. It is learning mastery over your thoughts.

To be happy, you must be able to perceive life as real, not the fuzzy dream many experience. To be focused, practice doing one thing at a time or thinking one thought at a time. Make your meditation active and alive in the moment. Walk, talk, sit and move consciously. Be aware of how every inch of your flesh feels.

Meditation is an experience of total aliveness. In meditation you learn to slow the thought processes down until you actually experience authentic meditation.

Concentration Gives Birth to Meditation

Meditation and life are one. When we are tumbled around by life, receiving all its bruises, it is shaping us. It is the rubbing and tumbling of life that polishes us. If we want to open up to new vistas of being, we must be challenged and sculpted. Concentration is one of those areas to polish. Your concentration deepens as you attempt meditation. Your breathing slows considerably. Those who meditate have lower pulse rates and their breathing becomes gradually quieter and less frequent. The more you control the breathing, the slower your heart beats.

Spirituality: Meditation

In true meditation you have entered a state of human hibernation. In this coma-like state there is one startling and shocking difference: You have reached the ultimate zenith of wakefulness. Never can you experience such aliveness while at the same time fighting against the drugging effects of the thought process. Just as in hibernation, the breathing and pulse are almost nonexistent. A knife or a needle could puncture your skin and you would not flinch. If this is not the case, forget meditation until you have mastered counting your breaths without a disturbing thought.

If you cannot go to a dentist and have a tooth filled or pulled without medication, you must go back and master step one of concentration. If, in this life, the only thing you ever accomplished was laser-like concentration, you would have reached a high plateau indeed. One last caution. Stay away from anyone who claims to have a secret technique or a magical mantra or any other mystical and hidden rite. Just as in the physical world, in the spiritual world there ain't no free lunch. If you are attracted to wild claims of weekend enlightenment, then you are either too lazy or too flaky for an authentic master to waste his time on you.

*Let everything you do
in this life be sacred
and every act spiritual.*

Concentration to Superconsciousness

As has been suggested: For superconsciousness, one must stay in a state of complete meditation; that is, a state undisturbed by a single thought for approximately twelve minutes. At this point you will have more control over your physical body and material world than you ever dreamed possible. Of course, this experience of superconsciousness is reserved for one person in a blue million. But don't let this discourage you. Just to be able to control your mental processes in concentration gives you 95 percent of complete control over your physical, emotional, material and financial world coupled with longevity known only by a few. It's not a bad place to be.

The key is for the mind to be trained not to drift. Cut out the distractions and your memory will increase to phenomenal proportions as well. Focus on one thought, then one word, then the spaces between the letters and then nothing at all.

Eventually you're bathed in the glorious, creative light of life's very Source.

Meditation Is Complete Control Over Our Mental Reality

Consider consciousness as if it were a beautiful blue sky. Inevitably a thought will appear. Immediately turn the thought into a visualized, small, white, puffy cloud and concentrate on seeing it dissolve. Once again, you are back to a state of clear, blue consciousness.

Once you start to exhibit control of your mind, you will start to control your reality on earth. No worries, anxieties or poverty. No illness, no apprehension and no debt, for now you know eternity.

Meditation will help us to be aware that what we think each moment creates our reality. There is no magic pill, only a journey that is straight uphill. When we control our thoughts, we have the key to greater dimensions. We can then go into meditation.

Learn to Be Quiet

Being in the world of nature provides an opportunity for a state of meditation to take place. Nature gives us great feedback. Take long walks by yourself or go on a canoe trip. Learn to be quiet and spend more quiet time alone.

Go searching for the taste of meditation. The right music can help, especially music played in the largo tempo, which has a beat similar to the human heart. Meditation means being really alive and experiencing that which is possible. Meditation is being totally in the moment. Only in meditation can we "explode" and open up to greater depths of consciousness.

At some point you'll realize why meditation has been sought for thousands of years by sincere seekers. We enter it simply, but come out of it with great profundity.

*Catch the scent and the flavor of life.
Living and being alive is what
it is all about.*

Look at a Flower or a Sunset and See It for the Very First Time

Plato looked at a flower and a sunset and "saw it for the first time" and knew nothing would ever be the same. Socrates tells of the first time that he really saw the stars. You can be so at home and so at peace once you begin to "see for the first time." For this to occur, you have to get the crowds out of your head and yourself away from the crowd.

When you walk, consider it a grand, sacred privilege. Feel the way your feet touch the ground. Learn to focus on your walking and let that be a form of focused meditation. There are chakras in the bottom of the feet, just as there are in the palms of the hands. The flow of these energy centers can be affected by being intensely conscious.

Consider an old martial arts exercise in walking. The student, when ready, is asked to walk and perform on delicate rice paper without tearing the paper or making a single noise by his movement upon it. That's how we should walk.

Play with Different Meditations

It is said that there are 108 different meditations, but that only one meditation is particularly suited for any individual. The "ancients" believed that it was the master who could select the one meditation for the student.

One meditation exercise is to listen to the nerve energy between your ears. Follow the pitch. It is a musical tone you can follow to its source which is beyond being audible. It is the soundless sound.

Whenever you concentrate, your breath slows. It's like when you thread a needle and hold your breath with concentration. Your eye movements will become focused and this in turn slows the thoughts. Finally, the breath stops.

At the deepest levels of meditation there is no need for breath. The heartbeat diminishes until one cannot find the pulse and you are ultimately still for a certain duration of time.

Play with different meditations. One technique will feel better than another. Musical people will be drawn to sound. Artists are drawn to a meditation using the eyes. Physically oriented, kinesthetic people focus more on body-oriented meditations.

The Positive Power Surge

The power of intention is, in fact, the power of spirit or motive force. With the right intention, we can have incredible power surges of energy throughout our bodies. You may have a power surge when sitting in meditation or when incredibly focused on an activity. The surge may come in perfect stillness. Whenever it comes, simply understand it is a manifestation of the motive power of intention. It is only evidence of a far greater experience.

GOOD EXERCISES FOR BEGINNING MEDITATION:

Bee in Hand Meditation

First, hold the hands together in a prayer position. This will create a magnetism between the palms. Put your thumbs together over your thymus gland

and with the fingers at the chin, focus your thoughts on the sound of a honeybee at the third-eye area. Begin to tap the thymus gland and make a sound like the buzzing of a honeybee, all the while focusing your awareness on the sound. When you can do this without being distracted, you will find that you have created such magnetism that it is hard to pull the palms apart.

The Om Meditation

One technique to clear the mental cobwebs is to vocalize the sound "OM". Repeat it 108 times and draw out the resonance. That is the number of beads on the Indian mantra rosary. The OM sound is like a psychic vacuum cleaner. The electromagnetic storms get cleared from our auric field when we sound the "OM."

The Candle Flame Meditation

Focus on the center of a candle flame. The periphery will darken and disappear. Soon the body of the candle will disappear, leaving only the flame. If your concentration is intense, you will feel yourself being magnetically drawn into the flame. If you envision the ancient symbol of the snake swallowing its own tail you will get a glimpse of this feeling. When you do this correctly, it can feel as though you're riding a motorcycle a hundred miles an hour through a small tunnel.

The Lover's Meditation

As two people sit facing each other, gazing into each other's eyes in an unblinking manner, a strange unity begins to unfold. Continue gazing and, at some point, the eyes will disappear and only one consciousness will exist. At that moment you and your lover are no longer — you have both melted into divine consciousness, into God.

The Mirror Meditation

Try this exercise by yourself. Stand and look into a mirror and gaze unwaveringly into your own eyes. Do not blink. Look into both eyes equally. Keep steady, without flipping back and forth between one eye and the other. When the eyes are static and the energy is intense, it must move, so it jumps into the pineal gland. It takes many weeks and even months of practice. Each session should take between 30 to 45 minutes. Most people however will not persist this long. The eyes can get dry and feel uncomfortable, but this ancient technique calls for the person to keep them totally open without blinking. The requirement is laser-like attention, something most people lack.

As you repeat this during several additional sessions, parts of the body will disappear, then the entire body, and you will look into your face and only the eyes will be looking back.

Finally, you will disappear entirely; but before you disappear, your face will start changing and you will see different faces of your past lives. Then one day the mirror will be empty.

Note: The author and publisher accept no responsibility for reactions to any of these meditation techniques. Consult your doctor if you question the suitability of these practices. They are presented for informational purposes only. These are personal opinions about varieties of meditation.

Thread Together Your Gems of Wisdom

At bedtime, replay the day in reverse as if you were watching a film running backwards. Think back moment by moment through the entire day. If you make this a daily process you will begin to thread the memories together. You will go further and further back into time and eventually even past your birth experience. The odd result of doing this is that you'll be able to see all this mental stuff as more and more illusion; not that it didn't happen, but the thoughts we use to see the past are the same thought materials we use to imagine the future. Soon we realize that reality is beyond thought.

Pull the mental thread and you'll be able to follow it to its source. Concentration is like pulling a thread; it requires focus and action.

An exercise you can do is to watch the seconds go by on your watch. Breathe in and listen and focus on those seconds. It's a simple exercise to develop the power of concentration. Do this several times throughout the day for one minute and then build it to five minutes. Watch the second hand go around and listen to your breathing. When you are able to do this successfully for five minutes without any extraneous thoughts whatsoever, you will have tasted meditation. In the meantime, you have experienced your power of focus to such a great degree that concentration has been developed.

Great Concentration Leads to a Great Memory

Look at something and concentrate. Memorize something by seeing it. Be aware enough to see it first. We learn to concentrate and develop our memory by first hearing, then by listening. You must consciously hear a person's name by listening to it. Work on your memory daily.

Memory is a remembrance of facts and events. Meditation is the suspension of fact and events. Concentration and meditation enhance your life.

Choose to Affirm Life

Choosing that which is life-affirming becomes an early form of thought awareness. During the early stages of thought awareness, you start qualifying your thoughts. Thought awareness takes training. Anyone can do it if they put one foot in front of the other.

Worry is not life-affirming. Worry thoughts, such as anxiety, lead to hypertension, heart disease and death. Choose today what you will serve, life or death. Which thoughts do you allow? Do you allow worry thoughts? If a scraggly motorcycle gang rolled up to your house — would you just invite them in? What about your negative thoughts that rumble up; would you meekly invite them in?

You have to first learn to distinguish between life-negating thoughts and life-affirming thoughts. Start with that first. Get into clear-thinking and contemplate meditation later.

Gratitude Is the Alchemist

Be grateful in all that you do. Even our meditations need to be regarded with gratitude. Focus on the light with thoughtfulness and reverence. Without light all is darkness.

Whatever it is you are doing, make it one-pointed, and it becomes a one-pointed meditation of life. Meditation is an act of gratitude for being fully alive. Do not meditate to become a zombie and to escape!

When we are grateful, the heavens shower down upon us. Be grateful. Focus on the flowers. Catch the scent and beauty of the rose. Live in brilliant, glorious and prosperous health, peace and love.

This Life Is So Good, You Don't Want to Miss It!

When each day is full of life — that juicy, that rich — you become the witness to all that happens in life. We're here for a while and then we're gone, but with enough of the fragrance of life, the scent lingers on. Life is so good when you learn to be the watcher, the eternal witness. The witness is you watching you. It is the best of you guiding the rest of you. It is watching over the treasure inside.

There is a wonderful story about a sage standing under a tree outside the wall of a mighty kingdom. The king would go out each night and sur-

Spirituality: Meditation

vey his kingdom. Every night he would see this strange man standing under the same tree. The king could no longer contain his curiosity and asked the man what he was doing. The man said, "I am watching." The king replied, "Oh, I am watching too. I am watching over my kingdom." To this the sage said, "You are watching over your kingdom on the outside, and I am watching over my kingdom on the inside."

Choose the inside kingdom. This is the life that can never be taken away. The richness within us can't be stolen. An authentic life surrounds itself with richness. Find a spot within that never fails. You will live without doubt in this place of certainty.

I am one with Thee.
I am in a state of grace.
The sound of silence is like your heartbeat.
I rest serene in your embrace.
I feel your hand. I see your face.
I live this day in grace.
I am one with Thee.

QUESTIONS AND ANSWERS

Tell us more about what the "OM" stands for and the history of this sound. How and when might one utilize it?

It is the basic creative, primal sound. It can be found in the roar of a well-burning fire. It is heard in the howl of the wind, the crashing of the waves and the tumbling of a waterfall. It is heard in the stillness of a remote mountain lake and it is felt as another desert sunrise begins. The sound that begins in silence also leads us in a return home, the holy OM. Deeper and deeper, beyond its hum another sound is found. It is a vibration like no other. OM was the word that created all things seen and unseen. Apart from that, nothing has ever come into being. Before the seas could move, before the earth could flower, this master worker was. It was the spirit that impregnated matter, the word gone forth to create. "In the beginning was the word, and the word was God, and the word was with God." (John 1:1)

As the deep-throated vibration roars from our heart cave, even the tactile nerve endings that run from the heart plexus to the cranial vault vibrate with such resonance that the cerebrospinal fluid massages the brain. The resulting neuropeptides then flood the body with the song of ecstasy, the new song, the sound of the heart, the anahata shabda. *The sound is so primal, so magnetic, so inviting and alluring. It is a wolf on a clear winter's night seeing the glory of the moon and the beauty of its fullness. Slowly and deeply the sound begins and suddenly it pierces the darkness and OMs from every direction join in chorus. As the myriad of stars light the night above, choruses of OMs illuminate the Earth herself. We, like the stars and Earth, are made of OM. Since we have traveled life the way of the prodigal son, we also come in full circle around again to the zero point, the empty circle, our home, the OM.*

A friend states that she likes to meditate with her eyes open, a Zen technique. She asks if you would recommend this technique?

Every waking moment can be a Zen technique, but we must be aware of its practice.

Meditation that allows detachment, just seeing, just awareness as if you were the world observing yourself, leads to the awareness that you are observing yourself.

The problem with closing the eyes for most people is that they tend to fall asleep. The problem with open eyes for most people is they tend to be distracted by what they see. Therefore, if you choose to meditate with open eyes, you will need to keep a universal visual focus. See everything at the same time, making no distinctions pro or con, just looking as if your eyes were empty and the universe with all its sights, sounds and smells were flooding into those two holes like a stream pours into a mountain pool. Then, at that point, you are the stream, the pool, the mountain and the earth that embraces it. You are the sky it scrapes and the universal envelope that holds it all. You are more and nothing at the same time.

Zen was born when Buddhism met Taoism and dropped the rituals. Zen comes from tea, the symbol of awareness. Bodhidharma, the grand patriarch of Zen, was said to have cut off his eyelids so he could stay awake. When, as the fable relates, he threw them on the ground, the first tea tree began to grow and thus, tea became the symbol of awareness. Ma huang has been used since that time as the meditator's tea because it helps keep your eyes open. Remember, many people have open eyes and 20/20 vision and yet see nothing because they are distracted. Practice seeing everything and being distracted by nothing and you will experience what you cannot ask.

The story about the man watching under the tree every night is beautiful. How can we become so committed and watchful?

There is a saying, "You cannot serve two masters for you will hate the one and love the other." Just as you cannot go in two directions at the same time, you cannot serve the ego-self and consciousness simultaneously. Few truly appreciate the enormous commitment required, and since the rewards of such intense vigilance appear intangible, motivation is always waning. My heart aches for those who, like moths, just flirt with the flame. Transformation requires jumping completely into the fire and being consumed and swallowed whole.

There is a tale of an ancient people who considered the ocean to be divine. They would gather each morning at sunrise to discuss the nature of this ocean god; but, since none of them could swim, no one dared to experience the water though they had decided someone should. Then, suddenly there appeared a man of salt, purposefully striding down a sand dune toward the surf. He said, "I will show you what God is like," and diving into the ocean he dissolved and never returned.

Who is next? Who has such passion for the unknown? Only a rare few. The others, in fearful panic of the thought, cling even tighter to their toys.

Seldom does one find anything profound on a T-shirt, but one I saw had a very truthful statement indicative of the majority of seekers. It read, "I've given up my search for truth. I'm now looking for a good fantasy!" I consider it sad and yet it is so very perfect; the greatest adventure available to a person is right before them and to take that road trip requires qui-

etude and stillness. Yet few comprehend this. When one is free of mental traffic, only then does the watcher appear. At this point one becomes the true seer, aware of the invaluable treasure of consciousness and the gem-like dazzle of beingness.

While the poor, rich king is fearful of losing his kingdom and must watch on the outside, he has no time available to go in search of a treasure he can never lose. No moth can consume it, no thief steal it, nor any rust destroy it. This kingdom, this treasure, can never be taken away once it is found.

Ah! the poor, busy souls seeking the next holiday, obsessed by the showy display of their means of life... the desire of the eyes and the filling of the senses are paramount. They never dream that as soon as it is attained, it is passing away like sand falling between the fingers, leaving only a new hunger in its place, a hunger that they once again must run to fulfill. To those who love that life, the love of consciousness is not in them. But to the one who stays awake and watches on the inside, that one endures forever.

Prune away those lifeless branches of senseless pleasures and vain activities so there may abound greater quietude. Within that space you may find the doorway to eternity for it is only in the absence of thought that the peace of God is found. Taste that and you'll never hunger again.

Will you speak to us about how to develop concentration, and its connection to enhancing our memory?

The very first thing to be understood about concentration is that it is a way we isolate a thought. When we isolate a thought, we are able to exclude other thoughts that distract us. In other words, we're able to focus on sounds, we're able to focus on the things we see, we're able to focus on that which we feel to the exclusion of all other distractions. Concentration requires an intense focus or awareness on one thing at a time. Often when we're introduced to a person for the first time, we do not remember their name because our head has distracted us. We have not listened carefully or focused our atten-

tion on the name being stated. Therefore, the name hasn't actually been heard consciously, and thus we do not have short-term memory retrieval of it even though we just heard it. We must hear the name before we can remember it, and that calls for concentration.

There are ways of making our concentration a visual image so that we're quickly able to identify things. It's almost as if we pegged one thing to another.

If you were in grade school and your teacher was asking the class to memorize the Great Lakes, you might think this to be a monumental thing to do. But I'll show you how to memorize and recall them at any given time with one simple image. Think of the image of homes sitting on the shore of a lake. All of us know how to spell "homes." Now, think of the names of the Great Lakes: H = Huron, O = Ontario, M = Michigan, E = Erie and S = Superior. At any time in the future the image of "homes" sitting on the shore of a lake will instantly remind you of the names of the Great Lakes.

We used our concentration to focus on an image. We then took the image and made it a peg and then utilized those pegs to relate to the names of the lakes.

If someone were to ask you the height of Mount Fuji, you could start by thinking of a year having twelve months. Then ask yourself how many days there are in a year. You know there are twelve months to a year and 365 days in that year. When we relate this to Mount Fuji, recall seeing calendars that picture this mountain in Japan. Imagine this beautiful mountain on a calendar which is 12,365 feet tall. It is a very simple way to remember the height.

First we've concentrated on a mental image and with related images we've pegged to the memory what we want to recall. Thus, concentration leads to memory.

When the concentration becomes laser-like, you'll be able to remember things that are far deeper and more profound for the spiritual aspirant. You can even remember coming out of the birth canal and the various traumas you experienced, thus allowing you to unravel the psychodramas that create problems in your behavior and that program you in later life. You can utilize your concentration to create a great memory, allowing you to recall the mundane or the profoundly significant.

There are so many memory systems being popularized today. Could you recommend one of those to help build our power of memory?

There is only one memory system and one alone that is valid and truly works. It is a system that goes back thousands of years. It is one that Aristotle, Plato and Socrates used. It was taught by the Pythagorean school yet it is one that goes far beyond Pythagorus, ancient Greece and Egypt. It goes back to the very start when people first walked upon this Earth.

This system is called the system of mnemonics. I would suggest that anyone who would really like to improve their memory to incredible proportions first learn the mnemonic alphabet. It's as simple as that. Based on mnemonics all other memory comes into being.

You cannot learn the mnemonic alphabet without concentrating, so I would recommend you use some of the simple exercises that have already been outlined, like being able to concentrate on the ticking hands of a clock for a minute without distracting thoughts. Or, simply to count your breaths.

Once you've learned the ability of unwavering focus, you will pierce the conscious mind into the deeper recesses of the subconscious and illuminate those as well.

Transformation

**There Must Be a Pruning So
We Can Become Our Ultimate**

For any orchard to prosper, there must be a pruning of the fruit trees so they can produce fruit. When the tree is correctly pruned, all the unproductive branches are cut so that the light can get through. When you are completely available to the light with no conflicting interests, you can see perfectly how your energies can be channeled in productive areas and not wasted on the frivolous and petty.

If you could see an expert orchardist prune, you would have implicit trust in him because you would see the visible evidence in the bountiful harvest produced.

We must prune not only our beliefs but also our habits and associations in the light of rational self-interest.

What Are the Roots of Your Habits and Beliefs?

Have you examined the roots of your belief systems, beliefs which give birth to your behavior, thoughts and emotions? Everything that you experience is a result of your root beliefs. In order for you to be happy, you must free yourself from irrational speculations and compulsive behavioral patterns. Pruning is essential. Deep inside, you want to learn, but your old belief systems battle you. Examine each behavior and belief to see if they bear fruit in your life or simply drain you of energy. Replace the fruitless with the fruitful.

We Are Receiving New Wine and It Must Ferment in Our Being

Find those teachers around you who have embraced the teachings of the new wine. Jesus said not to put new wine into old wineskins. The old wineskins have become inflexible, like many people's religions and beliefs. Provocative questions or new insights would stretch them to the breaking point very quickly. During seminar times we are receiving "new wine," and it must ferment within our beings. During the expansion process of this fermenting state, there is a sense of turmoil. The electrical field, the aura, is the "skin" of your soul that has to be strengthened to become powerful before it can expand and contain the light.

The new teaching must be contained for seven years until each cell has had time to restructure. The cells must release the old teachings and replaced them with the new. As we are infused with the new wine, the wineskin is transformed by the pressure. As the electrical field of our aura changes, our hands, face, and body postures change. Body changes occur with the embracing of new teachings. New beliefs can even change the shape of your skull.

The teaching of the new wine is what Peter calls spiritualized morphogenesis, or the rebirth of the purebred beings.

The Seed for Growth Is Found in Turmoil

There is a seed of equivalent benefit in all turmoil. Always there is a seed for growth during tumultuous times. During such times we realize that teachings are handed down from wineskin to wineskin (energy field to energy field). The copy is passed — the blessed teaching.

In the parable, Jesus is saying that as the new wine ferments and expands, it will burst the old wineskins that can't hold the new. They have become rigid. Jesus' teachings were new only in the sense that the population had never heard these ancient teachings before. They were bubbling and expanding and divine with light, and they expanded even the cellular memory.

Your body and your mind are bags of old memories that must be dropped, otherwise the new teachings and emotions and the resulting energy will burst your old self and nervous system. As we develop new thoughts, ideas and concepts, our images of ourselves change and thus new flesh ensues. As we drink of the new wine, we become transformed. We must be physically strong enough to carry this electrical current or charge in our energy field. The nervous system must be strengthened to hold the new teachings, the new energy.

We are each beautiful. We each transform as we grow, develop and expand. We are given that which we need at any given time for this growth. Always remember in life that which is essential, that which is important for you.

The path to the peak is arduous but it has always been that way. It is the path of truth through the valley of lies. That's why the mountain is so steep. But only from the vantage point of the peak can one truly see.

Release your past programming. Change your self-concept and your mental programs by doing the following:

1. Create an idealized "winning" self-image.
2. Take an honest look at who you really are and accept the truth about yourself.
3. Value what you find worthwhile about yourself.

The Moth Comes to the Flame

We need ideal images to climb toward. As we improve our self-concept, our performance improves. As we continue to expand our self-concept, we gain greater talents and abilities — more than we ever dreamed. Hold the vision of balanced perfection.

The way you are now doesn't change in the twinkling of an eye. Remember, by the inch it's a cinch, by the yard it's hard. Know that you are always in control of your growth pattern; realize that you grow by putting one foot in front of the other. When the idealized self, the real self and the positive self coincide, you are well on your way up the mountain. The moment you see yourself on the path up the mountain, you know you'll get there in time.

The path is straight up a stainless-steel mountain with no handholds. It's straight up, right before you, and you know where the peak is. When you know what you are looking for, you know where to find it. The trail will always be there. It takes dedication and desire.

Spirituality: Transformation

Take the Middle Path

Don't be too tight or too loose, but right in the middle. Sometimes the students who are initially the strongest are the ones who flake off the quickest. You can't be too tight or too loose; be tuned just right to be in balance and in the center.

Take personal initiative and apply effort in clearing out the old. Make your "container" strong and flexible in beliefs, and drop the old ways. Be flexible, sincere and conscientious but not so serious.

When you've worked all day, you can relax and let it be done. The same occurs with hard spiritual work. Do the preparation and then, when you relax, it happens.

Be patient and allow yourself time to change. Where you want to go is more important than where you have been.

The luminous life is not about information, it is about transformation.

QUESTIONS AND ANSWERS

Would you tell our readers your experience with the old orchard keeper? It illustrates so well how there must be a pruning in our lives before we can be our ultimate.

Certainly. Once I had a small orchard of several hundred apple, pear, peach and cherry trees. They looked like a beautiful procession of bridesmaids, all adorned and attired in pink and white blossoms, standing in rows and gently swaying on my hilltop cathedral.

Each spring they would don their flower dresses, but later at harvest time, they were relatively barren.

So, I sought out a master. This old orchardist always had thousands of richly bearing trees in the fall. The day we went to the orchard was a cold, wet, early spring morning. The cold fog made me shiver. We walked to the orchard and set a ladder up at the first tree. The old orchardman began his work — chop, snap, chop, snap. Soon the ground was littered with brush — and the tree more naked than the coldest winter wind could ever make her look.

I felt my heart sink. Seeing my graven look, he smiled gently and said, "Be not dismayed. It's not what we take up, but what we give up that makes us rich. The secret is emptiness. If I can pass a football through the tree without hitting a branch, then she is empty enough to bear richly in the fall. The chopping and cutting are only to rid her of branches that would later rob the life force of the taproot and leave her barren."

John, that day I learned a powerful teaching. Most of us clutter our lives with ten thousand things and vex ourselves by heading out in ten thousand opposite directions. Then we wonder why we bear no fruit in our lives... Hmm, strange isn't it? All we have to do is cut the branches.

Why do we all tend to go, as you say, in ten thousand directions?

It is because of a lack of focus, a lack of commitment and a lack of trust. Consider, if you cannot trust yourself then who can you trust? A master? No! Doubt will always be there. And when the master says "cut," you will run and your heart will sink in your chest. You will seek out another teacher who will not be so severe with your fruitless branches, and you will remain barren for yet another lifetime.

Would you talk to us a little bit more about how we all can live the luminous life?

Living the luminous life is not about information, it is about transformation. It is not about knowing more about things or just being more knowledgeable; it's having a knowingness, and that's totally different.

To live the luminous life implies that we live a bright life, one filled with light. The symbolism of this light is that it reveals things to us. It shows us exactly what is there. It illuminates.

The quest is, how does one live the perfect life? The perfect life cannot be lived without consciousness, and consciousness cannot be developed without concentration: concentration, focus and awareness. Being acutely aware every moment, every minute, every hour, every day; that is the work at hand. The more we do to distract ourselves from that work the further we get from what we can call the luminous life.

If a person wants to lose weight, does he continue to go on eating and eating and eating, stuffing himself at every opportunity? Of course not; that would be insane. Likewise, if a person wants more peace in her life, if she's really on the quest, does she continue to add more and more mental baggage, more things to think about, more burdens? No, she attempts to unburden herself. That is part of the work; the spiritual work at hand is to unburden oneself.

It's like the man who took a trip around the world. He climbed a mountain to find an old sage he had heard of. Upon arrival, he found no furniture in the sage's home. A little puzzled he asked, "Sir, where is your furniture?"

The sage looked at him directly and asked "Son, where is your furniture?"

The young man replied, "Sir, I'm only a visitor here. I didn't bring my furniture along."

The sage smiled and said, "Yes, likewise. I'm only a visitor here. I didn't bring my furniture along."

The spiritual quest is much like that. It's

seeking to unburden, to simplify, to have less, because having less is having more. When our treasure is consciousness, we gain consciousness by having less.

It's what we give up that makes us rich, not what we take up. Whether those things we take up be mental or physical, remember that we become a slave to everything we have. We become a servant to those things that serve us. So, by having fewer and fewer things to serve us and by simplifying our life, we are free to live the luminous life.

Enlightenment

**One Day the Sun Will Shine
for the Very First Time**

Siddhartha, while sitting under the bodhi tree, saw the day star rising at dawn on the horizon, just as it had many times before, but that morning he "saw it for the very first time." Forever afterward, the young prince would never again be the same, having experienced the unspeakable. He became a buddha, an awakened one.

Socrates, while outdoors one cold, clear night, looked up at the stars and is reported to have said, "If this be death, more of it." He saw with sudden impact and total clarity the startling beauty of the universe he had looked at countless times before but had never truly seen until that night.

See this life in its true light, and you will see heaven for the first time. It is so simple, yet so far removed. You are already pure but are simply unaware. The lock on life's cage is broken and the chains and shackles don't work. You're free — and you always will be — once you actually push against the door. Freedom cannot be taken away once it has been discovered.

What Is Enlightenment?

No one can say what enlightenment is. Lao Tzu said, "The Tao that can be spoken is not the eternal Tao." A mystical, ancient legend has it that the body fills with light and the eyes show it.

When you are always happy, free of anxiety or discouragement and life is working for you, it indicates that something must have happened!

A person who is awake will know how to use the mind and its ability to focus attention. Your mind, when directed, is your greatest protection and tool, yet enlightenment is beyond such basic, rudimentary, mental concepts.

When a person becomes enlightened, everything — people, animals and birds — all know it on a deep core level. But how can an unconscious person know if someone is a buddha? They can't until they become one themselves, and then nothing can be said.

Enlightenment Can Never Be Stolen

If enlightenment could be given to you, it could be taken away from you. You can't earn it, you can't buy it. It can't be given, and it can't be taken away.

You already possess enlightenment as your spiritual heritage, so you must attempt to discover the divine stage where it resides. It is in living fully and consciously that you discover enlightenment.

The nature of someone who has attained enlightenment is to live life as it is. Enjoy the sun when it is sunny, and when it rains, enjoy the rain. Life isn't such an arduous task! The secret is simply not wanting life to be some other way.

A shift in consciousness is required, and it takes a moment of intense awareness. We are either conscious, or drugged by our own thoughts. Remember, this powerful truth is always before us. How many of us are just dreaming that we are awake?

Peter would encourage us not to work for enlightenment. He would say to just stop resisting and fighting with life and then be ordinary for the first time. Relax and just be yourself. Just be yourself, be your essential essence. Forget about enlightenment. You'll be shocked at how fast your enlightenment is discovered.

We Are Light in Slow Motion

According to the world of quantum physics, we are light in slow motion. Our spiritualness, our light, has become embodied in matter. We are spiritual beings having a physical experience. Our physical experience can be filled with tremendous energy when our mind and our inner eye are focused on the summit, especially when we realize we are not locked in matter without being able to find the key for our release. When we do, only then do we know where we've been and where we're going.

When we focus on the summit, the light jumps to the third eye. Jesus referred to this as the "single eye." Jesus said that if your eye were single, your body would be full of light. A light in the eyes shows that someone is "home." If you are one-pointed in your intention, the eyes' light floods your "house." You start to enliven and enlighten.

When our eyes are held steady, an electrical spark jumps from the eyes, and the energy flows to the pineal gland and we start to illuminate. It is the pineal gland, an almond-shaped gland, that is believed to be a light receptor. The pineal gland catches the energy contained within the vibratory wave fonts of life.

When we are focused, the body is charged with energy. The body cells vibrate at an accelerated rate somewhat like a powerful, smooth-running dynamo. When we have total honesty and a passion for the truth, there is an energy transfer to the medulla oblongata, the pineal and the pituitary glands.

The Peace of God Occurs When the "Three Wise Men" Come

The Three Wise Men metaphysically represent the top three chakras — the fifth, sixth and seventh. The gifts they bring, frankincense, myrrh and gold, symbolize peace and love, the jewels of clairvoyant sight, and a rich inner wealth. That is what happens when those three centers open. The "inner eye of Jerusalem" is activated. (Jerusalem means "God's peace." *Jeru* means God and *salem* translates to peace.) The chakras are powerful energy centers that are often related to physical, glandular and nerve-center plexuses. The fifth, sixth and seventh centers are associated with the thyroid, pituitary, and pineal areas, and finally with the soft spot on the crown area of the head. The true crown of life is reserved for those who have conquered temptation at all levels. Only then do you become a king of kings, your kingdom a high spiritual realm, one far above earthly things. Your nervous system literally changes and is strengthened so that you can be a greater receptacle of prana or life force energy. When you increase the current like this, you will begin to glow energetically.

Spirituality: Enlightenment

There Is an Evolution to the Luminous Life

As you move along in the evolutionary process, you climb through various progressions. A lot of people in the spiritual community are neurotic; that is, some people become obsessed with fantasies and phobias concerning the spiritual quest and never embark upon a program with visual mile markers that will help determine progress in a rational manner. They can't get to the "seventh level" because they don't know the next step to take in their daily living. For one thing, you have to have a body to get to the seventh level. It is a sacred privilege to be in a physical form. But if you don't know the rules, the sacred privilege becomes a straightjacket.

You must start on the first rung of the ladder. There must be a mastery of physical survival which calls for money, exercise, and being in control of yourself, your emotions and your environment. It calls for being comfortable with the body, feeding it nourishing food, and providing it with shelter. Our basic needs must be taken care of first.

It doesn't take great intelligence to understand the law of cause and effect. Your vision of freedom or enslavement is based on the conclusions you've drawn from earlier experiences, and your reflection on what the actual causes were that created the wanted or unwanted effects.

A Pure, Enlightened Being Finds It Impossible to Suffer

In the beginning we were pure and fine, but the mind took on layers and layers of dross; thus arose the need for refinement. Only veils hide enlightenment within us. With "hot fire" experiences over long periods of time, the dross is removed and we become like refined gold, pure and 24 karat. At this point of refining, there is no more suffering.

A lifetime may be spent stripping away the veils, but underneath we all have the golden or gem-like qualities available to be polished. When our rough edges get rubbed away, we become more valuable.

A personality is generally classed as being very active, very inactive or somewhere in-between these two extremes. Only when perfect equilibrium is obtained is knowing the self possible.

Our real presence could be compared to a big jungle cat. It lies relaxed but is always watching. It knows exactly how to regulate its energy; not overactive, not underactive. We have to take time to slow down so we can be filled up with light and spirit and energy.

Peter says, "We must understand how to regulate our energy fields. Only from a center point of balance, or a satvatic position, can we begin to dig deep within our own golden mind. Only after a long time do we notice that the shaft we have dug opens to reveal infinity."

The Kingdom Comes as a Thief in the Night

The most enlightening thing to do is to forget about becoming enlightened. Just be that which you are in totality. You are free and always have been, except for the bondage of your thoughts.

When you least expect it, something wonderful happens, an unexpected experience occurs, and afterward you do all the same things, but now everything appears different. This universe hasn't changed, but because you have changed, it is all seen differently. In that culminating peak moment, you meet your soul mate face to face and that soul mate is you. You gaze into your own eyes and see only the light. The light seeks itself and you have a merging of who you have been with who you have become. Who you were is no longer.

In that culminating peak moment, you meet your soul mate face to face and that soul mate is you.

QUESTIONS AND ANSWERS

It appears to me that many people pretend to be enlightened. You say, however, that many are enlightened and pretend not to be. Would you clarify?

I only say that to indicate that God is not far off from anyone. Or said another way, your nature is buddha nature, your mind, buddha mind. Pretense, phoniness and inauthenticity cover the real self with a basket. When Jesus said, "don't cover your light with a basket," he meant, "be not false to any man." The inscription in Delphi was never more true and meaningful, "Know thyself."

This means we are not to confuse others or ourselves as to our true identity. When people say, "I am a CEO, a housewife, an actor, an artist, a doctor, a truck driver, etc." they are revealing what they do, not who they are. Those are simply masks that they wear. The difficulty has become — since people wear their masks even to bed — that they now believe the masks are their own true faces. The masks are "personas." The mask becomes the entire personality. Rip the mask off, and they can't bear the honesty of their nothingness. The fear is too much. Yet, they never suspect that the emptiness, the sunyata, *is their glory.*

The pretense of enlightenment is pretending to be what you have not yet realized that you really are. So you change your name, shave your head, dress out of character, adopt verbiage that appears to put you "in the know" (whatever that means) and run around trying to save others.

In the ancient world of Rome, there were countless sculptures. Many were flawed and patched up. Wax was used to fill the cracks and then they were passed off and sold as being sound. Of course, just like people when the heat is on, the false melts and the flawed original appears. So rampant was this phoniness that shops began to advertise with the words "sine sera," which meant, "without wax." It is from this we get the word "sincere."

Any fool can go around claiming to be enlightened. The institutions are full of these nut cases. Who stops long enough to ask, "Just what do you mean 'enlightened?' According to whom?" It's like giving a travel pitch for a place you can't find on the map. So you see, John, all I need do is turn up the heat, and we will all see where we stand.

Spirituality: Enlightenment

Are you enlightened?

John, how am "i" supposed to know?

Peter, is that a puzzle or a Zen koan?

Really, John, if you have to ask...

Peter, I am no longer looking for the Buddha.

A friend asks this question: "I have had moments of pure consciousness where I realize the intelligence and awareness of everything as a single wholeness. The experience is such bliss, I want only to stay there. Yet I cannot seem to exist there and in the workaday world of survival at the same time, and I lose that state of being far too quickly. How do you maintain such a state in the everyday world?"

If a person recovers from amnesia, do they forget themselves again?

Peter, would you tell us about your road to enlightenment?

I was asked this once before and because you too have asked me to share, I will. In 1978, I recovered from my amnesia. I then knew who I was and why I was here. My account was published in a book, Visions Eternal, *by Richard Oddo. Here is how I described it to Richard in 1991:*

When the dust of delusion clears from one's sight, there is the understanding that each one of us is, in our own little way, just a brush stroke on the great canvas of life. Some are bright, gaudy splashes of color, yet find themselves to be covered over by more subdued tints. Others may find themselves disappearing from the canvas altogether. Yet even the disappearance has left its subtle mark. We all have our personal story to tell. This is mine...

I am called by the name of Peter. This man called Peter is seen in many different ways. Some of the spiritually insensitive call him fraud, deceiver and fake. Others, with worshipful eyes, view him as saint or savior. The many colors I have been painted are the individual's own creation. Yet, is it not the same hand that paints us all? This splash of color known as the "Magic Man" has a heart that beats just like yours. I am an ordinary person who enjoys doing ordinary things, just like you. I have no more intention of courting the companionship of neurotic devotees, than of posing a threat to the egotistic who aspire to the status of world teacher. I have no answers to give except my love. Joy and laughter have replaced my questions. I have no healing to give except my presence. I am my own magic, freedom, love and bliss. I have no path to give — I have left no footsteps to follow.

Do you really want to read this? Your reading this is like allowing me to touch your eye. Can you see how intimate I would prefer this monologue to be? If you allow yourself to be open to what I am about to say, I promise I'll attempt not to press too heavily, for I would not want to blind you in the process. This is your story also, and the lines are all our own.

My beloved friend, who is my very heartbeat, has asked me to share the "Why" of enlightenment. Richard already knows the answer; I answer all the "why" questions about life the same way — with "because." I know, I know, you want me to get more specific. But my God, I have no idea! In a single flash of insight all my questions dissolved. That was just a few years ago or something like that. I could get really confused if for some reason I had to think about time, whatever that's suppose to be. Oh well, still there are a lot of close friends who can remind me.

Have you ever tried to describe how a particular, unusual food tastes? Strange, isn't it? You can only indicate. It's just like fingers pointing to the moon (by the way, don't bite my finger, it's only indicating a direction). Only *you* know the taste. Only *you* can reveal the sweet fragrance of something cooking in your kitchen.

I hear you, Richard, "Get personal, get personal!" OK, just for you. I'll tell why I started brewing this batch of nonsense. Sheer greed! A selfish, greedy lusting after inner peace. I was a pathological, religious fiend, foaming at the mouth while passionately reading every renowned holy scripture. This raving madman dragged this wretched bag of bones from temple to church to guru and back again. He had to save the world, feed the hungry, set the captives and prisoners free. A psychotic addiction for the approval of big daddy in the sky, or, for you folks who prefer a different gender, the holy mother.

Of course, I affectionately call her by another name. Am I pushing too hard yet? Are you ready to go to war against the antichrist or the demon king Ravana? Ah, just what we need, another good, bloody crusade. Oops, did I say that?

I really hope you're laughing as heartily as I am this very moment. If you are not, then you will recognize why your personal realization has escaped you. Seriousness is a cancer of the soul. From my own experience, I have found that sincerity and seriousness are polar opposites. Please just give me a moment longer before you blow your sadhana or make the "sign of the cross." Oh yes, I've seen hooded white saints, the true believers, burning crosses on the mountain. Hmm... something interesting about that. It's hard to dance with combat boots and helmets on. As I said in *The Magic Man,* wiggle someone's crutch of belief a little (playfully) and watch all their anger surface.

My dear friends, belief is not experience. Belief is a casket, and experience is the very juice of life. One day I laid all my beliefs down with the ashes of my religions. I was content to live in this rite of passage, this land of not knowing, this terrain of uncertainty and risk. Low and behold, all the demons of belief, status and respectability followed me into my personal wilderness. They taunted me; they pushed and shoved me in my unsteady space. They laid a banquet before me when I was starving. They poured forth their wine of delusion as I staggered to my feet. Then they viciously attacked me as I declined their poison-laden gifts. My escape from the world of religion and belief almost shredded my soul. But, the solace of knowing who you are heals any wound. I refused to eat at the table of hypocrisy, let alone be the very Passover lamb itself.

The chains of my beliefs were many, but so it is for woefully righteous men. I believed the sacred lies of others who had gone before. They said it was holy writ, the lineage, the brotherhood; and it was *the* unforgivable sin to disbelieve. What blasphemy! They said to venture beyond the confines of the known is to sail off the ends of the earth into the mouths of dragons. So be it! Let's get on with the death that knows no end. I'll get tan in the eternal fires of hell. I'll spit in the eye of the devil or dance with him. Who knows, it may be nothing more than an ill wind, a morning mist or a vapor on the sea of unknowing. And so it proved to be nothing more than a morning dew that was burned away by the dawning of the sun. All the fears that had kept me chained were only myths.

Have you ever noticed how children facing an unknown darkness react? They are in a panic for something familiar to hold onto. The blanket, dolls and pillows we as adults desperately grasp are only impotent illusions. These are the sugarcoated doctrines and other belief systems that lull the seeker into a deeper somnambulistic state. If you dream you are awake, how long do you suppose you will really sleep?

When you have the courage to enter the unexplored, unmapped wilderness of your own being, the first of many tests is complete. You must drop all preconceived ideas of what to expect. You must bring nothing of the past with you. For this to be a true rite of passage, you must go naked, hungry and honestly into that barren space. When you find your nourishment, an inner seed of power will begin to sprout. You become pregnant with enlightenment.

The day a decision was made to drop all my religious vows, teachings and ideas and enter life alone, was the day of baptism by fire and water. Burned were the bridges of the past and washed was the soul, free from the opinions of others. The harsh, new landscape started looking more like home every moment. I heard my own voice

say, "I have approved you my son, the beloved."
This voice echoed from a depth of consciousness
I had not known before. The realization struck
me, I was the father of my own being, son of my
own light, and self-approved. Some might think,
"Oh, how egotistical!" To those I can only smile
and quietly say, "Your judgment is your own
bondage. No one can be chained by it but yourself."

When one becomes content with "not knowing" life's answers, slowly, one realizes he never
really had a question. At that point an all-consuming powerful peace, an acceptance, enfolds
the growing embryo. A new birth is taking place.
The wilderness womb of your mother is not the
barren desert you once thought. Now one can
see that even the needled cactus has its flowers.
The scorpions, tarantulas and vipers were only
deadly thoughts and fearful dark imaginings.
This wilderness is now pregnant and alive! Those
who need to have answers also need to convince
others just so they can believe their answers to be
truth. From the safety of a belief system, and the
shield of a holy book, one preaches from the pulpit on the secrets of life, the virtues of being vegetarian and, of course, violent discourse on non-violence. Oh, and we can't leave out the topic of

Spirituality: Enlightenment

karmic retribution for all the unbelieving vermin who disagree with the only true way. Now I ask you, isn't that silly? What would possess a being to act that way? It is an old, worn-out, hand-me-down rag of doctrine, belief and opinion that one is supposed to wear, just because a body of elders pronounce it holy truth. Yes, the answers are so pat and smooth, the stories so appropriate. It seems no matter how skillfully the parrot tries to disguise its voice, it always gives itself away by that silly squeal.

When "not knowing" is pure, then love, truth and wisdom dawn automatically. When "not knowing" is pure, then knowing is the result. This may appear a paradox. This knowing has nothing to do with knowledge. This knowing gives birth to authenticity. An authentic being has no issues; he calmly goes about his life without concern. Authentic people need no banners to fly by, for they have their own rudders by which to steer. They are captains of their fate and masters of their soul. You will find a powerful authority in their speech. When they tell an ancient story or parable, it has become their own truth. They can never be intimidated by another's knowledge. They live in a knowing beyond words. Thus, you will never find them angry, bitter or cynical. Of course, this applies to anybody who claims to be a spiritual teacher. If that one is sneeringly distrustful of other peoples' motives, you can rest assured that they are not authentic, no matter how much they try to impress you with being totally open and straight. An authentic person is never such a wimp!

Authentic people are warriors who do not crumble at the contest of emotion. Even their physical presence tells you that they are lords of their world. They are too strong to whine or grovel at the feet of another. They are not thrown for a loop by the simple vicissitudes of life. They are not bitter weaklings who fall prey to gloom and despair in personal challenges. They even pay their bills, if they were to incur any, for their word is an unbroken truth.

They are warriors supreme, and challenge is their watchword. They are the very center of peace in the eye of the storm. When physical death stands before them, they laugh and say, "You should have come sooner — the joke is on you." "What do you mean?" asks the Grim Reaper. The warrior answers, "You should have come before I died; now who is having the last laugh?"

How does one die before they die? Could it

be that death and birth are the very same scent? Perhaps there are exceptions; after all, the universe is always full of surprises. There is one thing that I can say for certain: There is life before death in this incarnation, but you must die before you can enjoy it. This is not a physical death as such. It is more like a soul death (and I am not saying that the soul dies; it just feels like it). I cannot put this into scientific language any more than I can prove it. I can only try to share with you what happened to me. Please, just place this into your "for what it's worth" department, for, of itself, it has no value to anyone. You can't buy it, you can't sell it, you can't smoke, sniff or snort it, so forget it!

Here is the story. For twenty years I had engaged myself in severe spiritual disciplines and sacrifices. I worked only enough to provide basic necessities. I treasured the time spent in late-night prayers and morning scripture study. As the years progressed, I would meditate until two or three in the morning (I really just slept in a half lotus, which made my knees ache like hell). Then the morning would find me up around 3:30 to 4:00 a.m. for more sadhana. On some days I would do two to three hours of just pranayama and for several more hours chant mantras. God, I don't believe I'm writing this! Experiences, wow! Did I have experiences. Just about every spiritual experience that ever came down the pike. It was an hallucination extravaganza. I'm convinced now that the devil created all of this spirituality just to get his sadistic jollies. My enlightenment was about as far away as a salesperson for Brooks Brothers trying to sell a suit and tie to a native of the Amazon River. I was trying to sell the Divine on my worthiness for enlightenment. Of course, since I had my ears plugged with chants, mantras and prayers, I didn't hear God calling me a dumb ass. That didn't happen until some time later.

It happened early one morning. I had already abandoned all vows, spiritual practice and the like. Without reason, perhaps just by an old habit, I found myself before an enjoyable open fire. My expectations had died the past year or so. I really don't remember. All I knew was that I was alone, comfortable, with nothing to gain, sitting, enjoying the silliness of life. There were no serious thoughts about anything. I lapsed into no-thought. A strange light started bouncing up from my root center. Some may say it was the kundalini rising; if so, perhaps they may need to rewrite some of the texts written about the topic.

Spirituality: Enlightenment

With every bounce, the ball of light consumed more of me. My body turned to stone. The higher it rose the more I tried to resist. I was terrified. Yes, I have faced physical death many times in this life, and laughed in its face. But not this time; this was the death of everything I ever knew as myself. I did everything I could to try to stop it. Isn't that strange, that I would do that after all of those years of practice? When it was over, I heard off in the distance, as if in an echo chamber, what appeared to be myself say, "My God, it's real."

Now it's the same world, the same body and some of the same people I knew before. I still use the toilet, brush my teeth and bathe. I do more common things now than I did then, yet this world is not the same space that I left that day before the fire on that early morn. An obsessive egomaniac, with a compulsive, suicidal, serious vestige of a shell was burned to death in a splash of light, a white fire affair! My friends, I am here to celebrate the death of idiots and the birth of much laughter!

Epilogue: There is a Christ child of the heart in all, one who yearns to dance, sing and celebrate. A great master once said, "You will know the truth and the truth will set you free." This freedom can never be found in the head, nor can it be discovered in holy books or temples. Ceremonies, commandments and laws that were intended to protect us from the world have become the very walls of our own prisons. What a contradiction!

The enlightened one is the very Lord of the Sabbath, free from the biding restrictions of the fearful. We bring refreshment and rest wherever we go. It is the seventh day always, and life is our jubilee. We live in peace in the synagogue of the soul and worship no other gods but life itself, as it pulsates and beats in all that is.

And what is our identity? I am that I am, and so be it forevermore!

Conclusion

You may scope infinite vistas from where the Ganges is but a trickle, or breathe in deeply the virgin air of the Himalayas. You may scan the blue ocean's horizon while soft winds billow your sails, or leave your solo footprints on a soft South Sea island beach. You may exhilarate your soul by standing near the spray of the falling waters of Niagara, hike the Pacific Coast Trail, explore the dense rain forest of the Smokies, stand on the terminus of her winding path on Mount Katahdin in Maine, or hike the snows of Kilimanjaro in Africa. You may have seen the Seven Wonders of the World, but if you have not seen them through eyes free of dust, if you have not seen them through the eyes of a sage, then the whole world is but a petty, crass ugliness and you would have been better off to have been born blind.

To the sage the vision of your eyes, your endless journeys, reveal but cheap counterfeits, glass trinkets and fool's gold compared to the reality seen without eyes and traveled to without feet or wings and experienced without the luggage of body and mind.

O! How vast and unspeakable, for I can only tremble as I contemplate her beloved glory, and the tears on my cheeks are for you.

The wheel eternal, in its relentless roll, crushes all. The spokes, like people, point first to this and then to that, to ten thousand objects which are never really seen. The tears of the sage wash the dust from the ten thousand illusions. The tears of the sage flow from the empty hub upon which the universe revolves. The sage, the seer, scopes the infinite vistas of the unspeakable realm and trembles... for the tears are for you.

- Peter

Don't miss —
Volume One of

The Moth Comes to the Flame: Conversations Between Seeker and Sage

Begin the spiritual journey with wisdom from Peter's seminars combined with his insightful answers to a seeker's questions.

Table of Contents, Volume One:

Life
The Luminous Life — What Living Should Be
Creating the Life You Want
Fulfillment Is the Gateway to Happiness
The Joy Is in the Purpose

Self
Seek the Truth
The Body's Radiance
The Magic of Self-Esteem
Finding Personal Freedom
What You Speak Is What Shall Be

Relationships
Mastering Relationships
How to Find a Good Relationship
Making a Relationship Work
Dealing with Difficult Relationships
Parents, Children and Other Friends

Emotions
Love
Courage
How to Handle Negative Emotions
Overcoming the Fear of Death
How to Cope with Change
How to Help Those Who Are Dying
Gratitude
True Peace

To order, specify Volume One ($20.00) or Volume Two ($25.00) or both plus $4.00 shipping and handling to:

> **Roaring Lion Publishing Company**
> **P. O. Box 471**
> **Boise, Idaho 83701**

Visa and Mastercard orders: 1-800-358-1929
(Idaho residents add $1.00 sales tax for Vol.I and $1.25 for Vol.2.)
($4.00 will cover shipping for up to two volumes.)

About the Author

John Roberts is a popular motivational speaker and seminar leader for both private and government agencies. He holds a Master's Degree in Psychology and has been a counselor and therapist for over 24 years in his native state of Idaho. Also a successful entrepreneur, John was the co-owner of Le Poulet Rouge restaurant and co-founder of the Moxie Java espresso shops.

John travels extensively throughout the country speaking on topics touched upon in his books, *The Fruit of Your Thoughts: Explore Mind, Money and Enlightenment*, and the two-volume set *The Moth Comes to the Flame: Conversations Between Seeker and Sage*. John has been faithfully attending seminars given by Peter since 1991 and has compiled this extensive information to make it accessible to others. He may be contacted at Roaring Lion Publishing Company, P.O. Box 471, Boise, Idaho, 83701.

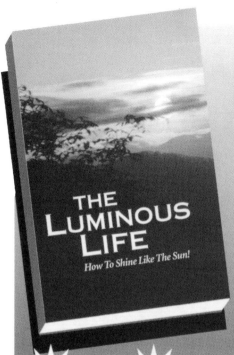

Ancient echoes will whisper within, joy will fill your heart with joy, and your spirit will sprout wings and soar! Here is a story to cherish! Here is a hope to embrace! Here is the book you have waited for –

THE LUMINOUS LIFE

420 pages, 6" by 9"
Retail price $20.00,
plus $4.00 S&H
Idaho residents add $1.00 sales tax.

For wholesale or retail orders, send check or money order to:

P.O. Box 471
Boise, ID 83701

or call 1-800-358-1929
MasterCard and Visa welcome

Also available from Ingram, New Leaf, and Partners

I asked Peter, jokingly, "What's this book about?" He just laughed and said "Everything from Jesus to skin care!" Even though these are my second and third books on his teachings, I still feel I have only scratched the surface, revealing a glimpse of an awesome void filled with deep silence.

A road map into the kingdom of the new consciousness!

Volume One, 368 pages, 5" by 7 3/4"
  Retail price $20.00 plus $4.00 S&H
  Idaho residents add $1.00 sales tax.
Volume Two, 488 pages, 5" by 7 3/4"
  Retail price $25.00 p;us $4.00 S&H
  Idaho residents add $1.25 sales tax.
Order both volumes, shipping total $4.00

For wholesale or retail orders,
send check or money order to:

P.O. Box 471, Boise, ID 83701
or call 1-800-358-1929 MasterCard and Visa welcome
  Also available from Ingram, New Leaf, and Partners

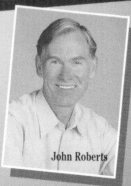

John Roberts

INSIGHTS OF PETER ROSEN

The Fruit of Your Thoughts

By John Roberts

EXPLORE MIND, MONEY AND ENLIGHTENMENT

Free yourself from useless bondage and the shackles of self-defeating beliefs. Reach high. The sweetest fruit ripens at the end of the limb where the sun shines the brightest, and it takes great courage to reach it.

The secret to inner peace is to be yourself...

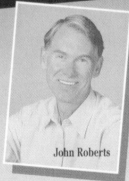

John Roberts

272 pages, 5" by 7 3/4"
Retail price $20.00,
plus $4.00 S&H
Idaho residents add $1.00 sales tax.

For wholesale or retail orders, send check or money order to:

Roaring Lion PUBLISHING COMPANY
P.O. Box 471
Boise, ID 83701

or call 1-800-358-1929
MasterCard and Visa welcome
Also available from Ingram, New Leaf, and Partners

Are You Ready?

We guarantee that your heart will overflow and you will be touched in a most unusual, delightful way as you read

Discover an enriching personal experience as you turn its pages. Your life will never be the same after reading THE MAGIC MAN,

Welcome home! Between these pages you will find: Spectacular color inserts; many powerful and unbelievable photographs; special interview with Peter, the Magic Man of Mystic Mountain; enchanting true life experiences, and a volume filled with the fragrance of enlightenment.

**126 pages, 6" by 9"
Retail price $13.00,
plus $4.00 S&H**
Idaho residents add $1.00 sales tax.

For wholesale or retail orders, send check or money order to:

Roaring Lion PUBLISHING COMPANY

P.O. Box 471, Boise, ID 83701

**or call 1-800-358-1929, MasterCard and Visa welcome
Also available from Ingram, New Leaf, and Partners**